proclaiming good news on special days

proclaiming good news on special days

resources for preaching on special days and occasions

Compiled by Harold Bonner

Contributors:

Eugene L. Stowe, Leslie Parrott, Bill M. Sullivan,
Oscar F. Reed, George E. Teague, H. B. London, Jr.,
Russell Metcalfe, Jarrell Garsee, Dallas D. Mucci,
Alan L. Rodda, Harold Bonner

BAKER BOOK HOUSE

Grand Rapids, Michigan 49506

Permission to quote from the following copyrighted versions is acknowledged with appreciation:

The Holy Bible, New International Version (NIV), Copyright © 1978 by the New York International Bible Society.

The Living Bible (TLB), © 1971 by Tyndale House Publishers, Wheaton, Ill.

The Bible: A New Translation (Moffatt), copyright 1954 by James A. R. Moffatt. By permission of Harper and Row, Publishers, Inc.

New American Standard Bible (NASB), © The Lockman Foundation, 1960, 1962, 1968, 1971, 1972, 1973, 1975.

New English Bible (NEB), © The Delegates of the Oxford University Press and The Syndics of the Cambridge University Press, 1961, 1970.

Revised Standard Version of the Bible (RSV), copyrighted 1946, 1952, © 1971, 1973.

Good News Bible (TEV), Old Testament © American Bible Society, 1976; New Testament © American Bible Society, 1966, 1971, 1976.

Contents

Preface

In the repeating cycle of the years, the Christian pastor comes again and again to those days and occasions where he has been before. The challenge is not simply to declare the gospel of Jesus Christ, but to proclaim it with relevance, clarity, authority, and freshness. That is not always easy to achieve, for the natural tendency is to see what we have seen before, to say what we have said before, and to do what we have done before.

This book is designed therefore primarily as a resource for pastors in providing new insights into preaching the Good News of the gospel on those special days and occasions that he faces in the course of the year. The selection of such occasions could have been larger or smaller, but the ones chosen are the major ones of the year: the dominant days of the Christian calendar—Christmas, the Cross, Easter, and Pentecost; the major themes from the national calendar—New Year, family and home, national holidays, and Thanksgiving; and some of the special occasions that present themselves in the course of the year—baccalaureate, communion, and funerals.

The format used here is the same as in two previous books, *Proclaiming the Spirit* and *Proclaiming the Savior*. Each writer presents a section in which he describes his concepts and goals of preaching on the occasion assigned to him, followed by the substance of four messages dealing with that theme.

I am deeply grateful to the distinguished men who have consented to write for this volume. To read them is to know again that for the Christian pastor, though there may be many special days and occasions, there is but one theme: "Jesus Christ, the Son of God who became the Son of Man, that sons of men might become sons of God."

—HAROLD BONNER

Proclaiming Good News
on Special Days

GEORGE E. TEAGUE is superintendent of the Upstate New York District. From 1969 to 1981, he pastored First Church of the Nazarene in Baltimore.

He is a native of Maine, a graduate of Eastern Nazarene College and of Nazarene Theological Seminary.

Previous pastorates include churches in New Jersey, New Hampshire, Maine, and First Church in Syracuse, N.Y.

Midway through his decade of leadership at Baltimore he led in a relocation program. Since that time the church has experienced excellent growth.

He has served as District NYI president and Church School Board chairman. The Washington District is the second district on which he has served as secretary. He is also a trustee of Eastern Nazarene College.

NEW YEAR

George E. Teague

Preaching on special days is one of the exciting challenges of the pastor. The historical events and traditions associated with these days provide material for the sermon which tends to get the attention of the listening audience as it is related to the text upon which the sermon is based.

New Year's preaching is especially challenging. Some pastors continue to relate their sermons to the theme well beyond the one Sunday designated as New Year's Sunday.

Preaching at the New Year is an excellent opportunity to share with an audience the encouraging truth that in Christ there can be a new beginning. A new year represents, in a sense, a new beginning. New life in Christ offers men a new beginning. The theme of forgiveness is a natural one for this season, as is the power of Christ which makes new. The New Year is also a time to look back over the yesterdays and evaluate one's effectiveness as a Christian. This quite naturally moves many to resolve that by God's grace, changes will be instituted which will make for greater effectiveness. From a study of Philippians 3, it is easy to believe that Paul would be in sympathy with this approach to preaching at this season.

There is also the need to allay fears of the unknown which is ahead. Most every man thinks about the possibilities of illness, financial reverse, change in relationships, development of crucial world conditions. What if life tumbles in during the New Year? The assuring words of the pastor based on the eternal Word of God will get a hearing from men who live in a world subject to shakings and whose little worlds are anything but immune from trouble. There are numerous texts for sermons on this theme. He is the God of all comfort who ordained that such words as these should be penned about himself: "God is our refuge and strength, a very present help in trouble" (Ps. 46:1).

The New Year's season is also an excellent opportunity to present truth which will give men confidence so that they can endure the race in which they are involved. In our congregations, there are those who are exhausted, fatigued, low on energy, negative in their thinking. They just about made it to church today. Can they make it through 364 more days? How exciting to think that it may be the pertinent, appropriate, Spirit-anointed sermon of a pastor which gives assurance that "as thy days, so shall thy strength be" (Deut. 33:25).

Another direction for New Year's preaching is the encouragement of members of a congregation to believe that they can, during the year ahead, reach goals which before have evaded them. The past does not need to provide a ceiling for the future. The new, unknown, untried year, under God, has unlimited potential. There is more power than what we have thus far experienced. There is more grace. Why not let this be the year when we draw upon His grace and power, as never before, and, as a result, realize the spiritual goals before us! A natural opportunity to motivate a congregation to new heights is provided through New Year's preaching.

This season also offers a splendid opportunity to deal with the disciplines of the Christian life. Many can be incited to start reading the Bible through at the beginning of the new year. Along with that there can be the challenge of getting into the Word and of developing a new level of effectiveness in prayer. Then, too, what about a new chance to share our faith, which chance most Christians feel they need in light of their track record.

A further New Year's approach is that of dealing with the theme of last things from the standpoint that this can be the year when the Savior who promised to come again will break into history for the second time. The resulting call is to living in readiness.

The pastor who capitalizes on the possibilities of New Year's preaching is using good strategy for overcoming the tendency toward loss of excitement and movement which is apt to be experienced throughout his congregation following the festivities of the Christmas season.

Time to Take Your Mountain

TEXT: *Now therefore give me this mountain, whereof the Lord spake in that day* (Josh. 14:12a).

It was now 45 years since Moses had selected a representative from each tribe to do an invasion feasibility report on the Promised Land. How strong were the people? Were the cities fortified? Was the land productive?

The report, from the standpoint of desirability, was most favorable. In fact, it took two men to carry a bunch of grapes from Eshcol. It was a land just flowing in milk and honey. Their cities, however, were fortified and there were giants in the land. There were only two "yes" votes on the question of invasion.

Now their trusted leader, Moses, had been succeeded by Joshua, one of the two reporting favorably. One day, Caleb, the other possibility thinker, stands before Joshua, and this is what he states: "Remember the mountain the

Lord promised me back there when we checked out the Promised Land? Give me my mountain; it's time for me to take my mountain."

Caleb was not the last man to whom God has made promises which have not yet been realized. To some of us, long ago, God indicated that He had some territory He wanted us to annex. Perhaps the first item on our agenda for the new year should be taking what God wants us to have, taking our mountain. We, too, have waited long enough. Where do we begin?

I. We Need to Recall That Which He Wants Us to Have

Not long ago I sat with a group of ministers in a very heart-searching session. We had been studying principles and procedures which would help us with our work when we got back home. At the moment, however, we were in process of listing some goals and objectives to be reached by the use of the techniques we had learned.

While it is easy to have some goals of our own choosing, I hope those ministers listed some goals which God had clearly outlined for them. I hope some things which were listed were items which God had talked to them about as being in His will for them before they ever came to the conference. Doubtless some matters listed had long been on God's agenda for them.

Could it be the same with you today? Right now, you can remember some times when you have had audience with Him, and He revealed to you some spiritual goals. How exciting! What a new dimension they could add to your life if successfully pursued! Perhaps He told you, "I want you to get into the Word, really get into the Word. Read it, study it, memorize it, share it." Perhaps He gave this impression: "I have new plateaus of prayer for you. Don't settle down on the low levels of this rewarding Christian practice. Move

14

up to where the air is clear and sharp and the vision is broadened." Perhaps His concern for you was that you would become a Christian able to share your faith more effectively. He assured you that He could use you way beyond your present level. You were excited, but you never took your mountain.

The early days of a new year could be a likely time to review the issues about which God has talked to you in the yesterdays and get them at the top of the agenda for the year just ahead.

II. We Also Need to Review the Obstacles to Conquest

The territory promised to Caleb was the Hebron area. Do you know who lived there? That's right, the Anakims. Not only did giant-size grapes grow there, but giant-size men as well. They lived in great cities which were well fortified.

It's tempting to call back across the centuries and advise old Caleb, "You had better forget Hebron. Too bad that this was the area assigned to you. Had it been another area, you might have taken it, but certainly not this."

There he stands, 85 years young, and declares, "I know all about it—giants and fenced cities—but I want my mountain!"

The problem is that many of us do not stand beside Caleb in this respect. We know about the obstacles, and we do not believe we can take what is ours.

What obstacles have inhibited your progress, kept you from your mountain? People, geographical location? Perhaps. Lack of discipline, insufficient motivation, lack of commitment, unwillingness to pay the price? More likely. The tendency to feel comfortable with the familiar and afraid of the unfamiliar? The unwillingness to admit that the past represents less than the best?

15

Are there any obstacles big enough to keep us from what God wants us to have? Did God not know that they were there when He promised, "This is what I want you to have"?

Why not list the obstacles and examine them carefully. Are they really big enough to deter you from possession? I doubt it.

The call is for men who, like Caleb, rehearse the obstacles, but in the next breath cry out, "Give me my mountain."

III. We Need to Renew the Spirit of Conquest

Why did Caleb, at 85, stand there before Joshua and cry, "Give me my mountain"? Because that's the kind of man he was; he was that kind of man 45 years before. He helped write the minority report which said, "Let us go up at once, and possess it; for we are well able to overcome it" (Num. 13:30). He was a possibility thinker from the beginning.

Perhaps the majority would have liked to slow him down a little during the years. Perhaps they halfway wanted to make a nonbeliever out of him, but the old spirit was still there.

Perhaps your spirit of conquest has diminished in recent days. Perhaps the urge is not there like once it was. Perhaps you are satisfied with what you have.

That will not do, however, if God has more for you. And you cannot be really satisfied if you have seen your mountain. You have no other choice; you must begin where you are and ask for a renewal of relationship which will bring a renewal of desire to have what He wants you to have. Caleb's relationship accounted for his spirit of conquest. He declared, "If so be the Lord will be with me, then I shall be able to drive them out" (Josh. 14:12b). His

16

presence makes us want what is ours and gives us confidence that what is potentially ours can be ours.

A new year lies before us. It's time to take our mountain.

This Year a New Year

TEXT: *Ye have not passed this way heretofore* (Josh. 3:4*b*; cf. 1-5).

There's a new year ahead, new according to the calendar, and potentially new in quality.

A resolution-maker and -breaker, in good standing for years, says it is considered very square these days to make New Year's resolutions. Perhaps, however, that's the very thing we ought to do—this in the interest of unrealized potential and unfulfilled possibilities. Why not make this year a new year!

If this is our aspiration, we shall be looking for a formula. Let me suggest one.

I. Impound Your Impediments

Somewhere I read of a lunacy test used by a trial lawyer in the yesterdays. He ordered the person in question to bail out a watering trough. Sanity was determined by whether or not the one being tested shut off the faucet before starting the bailing process.

A beginning place in the process of realizing new aspirations is that of dealing with those things which threaten to impede our progress; and they are there. Outstanding among them is the record of our yesterdays. Whoever talked about unborn tomorrow and dead yesterday was

17

unrealistic. I would agree with another who said of yesterday: "It is alive, vibrant, fecund, making today and shaping tomorrow." Unless we can find some way to care for the accumulation of the past, we shall be hindered in the future. Isn't that where Jesus begins with us—dealing with our past? That's a thrilling part of the gospel. Christ offers forgiveness. In fact, there is no other way to deal with yesterday.

The impediment of fear needs to be dealt with also—fear because of past failure, fear because of the unknown future, fear because of unforeseen possibilities. The Christmas story, fresh in our minds, depicts God as dealing with men's fears. To the shepherds, shaken by the appearance of an angel and the glory of the Lord which illuminated the area, the angel said, "Fear not" (Luke 2: 10). Then he told of the birth of the Savior, the continuing answer to men's fears.

There are also crippling emotional attitudes, stemming from the past, which strain relationships and rob us of the healing fellowship with others which we need so much. In Christ Jesus there is cleansing for these, for "if we walk in the light, as he is in the light, we have fellowship one with another, and the blood of Jesus Christ his Son cleanseth us from all sin" (1 John 1:7).

Numerous are the possible impediments with which we must deal if the days ahead are to be the kind of days we want them to be. The Savior is a specialist in helping us deal with them.

II. Plot Your Plan

There's a word which is used a lot in these days in the business world when effort is being made to enhance efficiency. The word is *strategy*.

Jesus told the story of the rich Jew whose steward had

bungled his assignment and was about to be fired. While not efficient in the management of his master's estate, the steward was shrewd in the rapid development of a strategy which would bring him benefit to compensate for his loss of salary. While his master's debtors thought he was still employed, he went to each one and changed the note, reducing it sizeably. This was a clever plan to incur indebtedness which would pay off later. His dishonesty was deplorable, but his clever strategy was commendable.

When asked his secret, a most successful 20th-century businessman replied, "Shrewdness." He indicated that every waking hour was spent thinking, scheming, planning, putting deals together.

There is so much failure, so much inefficiency, so much below-par Christian living. Why don't we Christians plan for success in the all-important venture of knowing and serving Jesus! The basics are there. The Bible is our Guidebook. Volumes have been written dealing with the strategy of living the life. Why don't we plot our personal plan in which we outline a program for personal employment of a working strategy for effective Christian living!

III. Seek Needed Strength

As we stand on the threshold of a new year, it's a good time to look back in an effort to discover in what specific areas we missed it. Such an exercise would reveal to many that their problem was failing to draw upon His power. His work cannot be done without His power.

One of the beautiful promises of the Word is so appropriate as we think of needed strength for the days ahead: "As thy days, so shall thy strength be" (Deut. 33: 25). This indicates that we do not have to live and serve in our own strength in any period of our lives, including the year ahead.

There's a Jewish legend that during the famine, Joseph commanded his officers to cast grain and chaff on the waters of the Nile so that the people down below, to whom the waters flowed, would know that there was plenty of food up above. We have reason to know that there is plenty of strength available from above. That's what we need to know.

So we find ourselves in the early days of a new calendar year. It is unblemished. It is pregnant with possibilities. We want it to be a new year. We want it to contrast with the past in many respects: failures, achievements, effectiveness in service. Follow the formula, and, under God, the contrast will be there. This year will be a new year.

New in Christ This New Year

TEXT: *Therefore if any man be in Christ, he is a new creature: old things are passed away; behold, all things are become new* (2 Cor. 5:17).

In answer to the question, Did you ever invite Jesus Christ to come into your heart? the slightly inebriated man answered, "Yeah, but I'm not getting much of a kick out of it now."

That suggests a big problem in Christendom, and a tragic situation in many lives. What happened back there isn't making any difference now.

There are many in whose lives this situation is being corrected. That's the reason for much of the new movement in many churches today. The factor which makes the difference is a present, vital faith in Christ which makes for a life-changing relationship. "If any man be in Christ" are the immortal words which convey this truth. We commonly think of this truth as relating to the initial conversion experience. We must not forget, however, that He continues to make us new only when we continue to live in relationship with Him.

Suppose it isn't making any difference right now, what then?

I. Recognize Your Failure

For five hours the other day we had no lights at the parsonage. It reminded me of that early evening a few years ago when, as I drove toward home following an afternoon of calling in an eastern city, I suddenly noticed that all the lights were out on the streets and in the homes. They call it power failure.

There's also a power failure in the spiritual area of life. The lights go out in the soul. There is the loss of spiritual energy and the resulting immobility on the spiritual thoroughfare of life.

It's a failure of which sometimes we are unaware until it has developed quite extensively. The reason is that we do not quickly depart from the Christian patterns of life which have been established. The appearance is much the same, but the essence is not.

It is always difficult to admit failure even though it becomes evident. Occasionally somebody does, and this is the first step in heartening change. There's the refreshing story of a pastor who was shown that he had neglected calling on the elderly of his congregation. The reminder hurt, but he admitted the failure. He began to give his attention to this area where he had been negligent. A most effective program of ministry to the elderly developed. That's suggestive of the way to begin to deal with our spiritual failure.

21

II. Reestablish the Relationship

It is no secret as to how the spiritual quest got started. It all began when, by faith, we established a relationship with Jesus Christ. He was the Source. It never happened until He entered our lives.

How do we get things going again? The answer is easy to find; reestablish the relationship. That will start again the inflow of the good things of the Spirit. He remains their Source.

A church member did that one Saturday morning when at home by himself. Results: Christ in charge of his life again, prayer a meaningful practice once more, what Christ can do through him the determiner of his reach, tenseness and tightness gone, Christ the Source of direction. The explanation is easy: "If any man be in Christ, he is a new creature."

III. Reinstitute the Disciplines

Most relationships with Christ go wrong at the point of failure to follow the disciplines of the new life. I am talking about being into the Word; we meet the Living Word in the written Word. I am talking about prayer, which is two-way communication. I am talking about worship with the Christian community. I am talking about sharing our faith with others.

There's only one way. We must decide that the relationship with Him is so vital that nothing will deter us from those exercises which keep it intact. We must determine that no price is too great to pay.

Bunyan in *Pilgrim's Progress* vividly describes a man with strong countenance looking at the price of life and then saying: "Set my name down, sir. For I have looked this whole thing in the face; and cost me what it may, I mean to have Christlikeness and will."

Ah, that's the stance that will keep Christian experience meaningful in this new year.

IV. Reconsider the Alternatives

The alternatives to keeping new in Christ are anything but attractive. It's true with a body of believers and on the individual level as well.

I could take you to a community where there is a lovely white frame building no longer used. I remember when there were at least three services held there weekly. Then there were two. Then there was one. Then none! The emphasis had changed until it was no longer a manner of knowing Christ and keeping new in Him. That kind of church does not reproduce; rather, it goes out of business.

The alternatives to keeping a nowness to our newness in Christ are also dismal for the individual Christian. The light goes out, the sprint in the step is gone, the inner joy has subsided, there is no faith to share.

Christ is the original Source of newness. He is the continuing Source. Keep new in Him this new year.

The Church for the New Year

Text: *That ye may be blameless and harmless, the sons of God, without rebuke, in the midst of a crooked and perverse nation, among whom ye shine as lights in the world; holding forth the word of life; that I may rejoice in the day of Christ* (Phil. 2:15-16a).

Several years ago, when our country was showing signs of economic instability, right in the heart of the nation there

23

was a pocket of prosperity. It was the booming city of Wichita, Kans., located on the banks of the Arkansas River. Its unemployment rate was 3 percent. It had a $14 million city hall under construction, and the board of education had just approved a $30 million building program. Right in the midst of a nation plagued with economic problems there was a pocket of prosperity.

What does our world need most as we stand at the exit of an old year and the entrance of a new year? Pockets of spiritual prosperity! Groups of dynamic believers scattered all over the place. Colonies of heaven living "clean, innocent lives as children of God in a dark world full of people who are crooked and stubborn" (Phil. 2:15b, TLB). That's the church, the way it was meant to be, and the world needs it to be.

What will enable a body of believers to be this kind of church?

I. A Consuming Passion to Know Christ Jesus

A well-known Christian motivator says there are two questions which he asks as he comes to a group to begin his work: "What do you want?" and "Where are your men?"

What do we want as a church? What are our goals? Fulfillment through service? Social opportunities? Exciting youth programs? Entertaining specials? What did Paul want? "That I may know him" is the way he put it (Phil. 3:10). He wanted to know Jesus better. He does not leave the impression in this chapter that his desire was mild and passive. It was a driving passion. It was knowing Christ at any price.

Now, almost 20 centuries later, this is still where the action is. There is no real spiritual life apart from a vital relationship with Jesus Christ. Perhaps the constituency in

24

many evangelical churches can be divided into two categories: those who keep the rules and honor their vows; those who, along with doing the above, seem alive and vibrant and whose lives clearly center in Christ. They seek Him, the Living Word, in the written Word. They talk about Him; it seems to come natural. They share Him; He is the best they have.

It is no surprise that they are the people who act spiritually alive. John explains it when he writes: "In him was life" (John 1:4). Jesus himself helps us understand. He says, "I am come that they might have life, and that they might have it more abundantly" (10:10).

A pocket of spiritual prosperity will be found only when there are Christians who have a consuming passion to know Jesus.

II. An Overflowing Love for Others

Paul was not only inwardly excited, he was outwardly motivated. He moved out to others in an impressive measure. The reason is no secret: Christ filled his heart with love for others.

We have heard a lot about love in these days, some of what we have heard not being too impressive. More impressive is the demonstration of love which Paul gives. Love in action. Love reaching out to others at great cost to himself. Love which got him in prison. Love which made him a target for stoning, resulting in a back which was bleeding. Love which, however, resulted in men everywhere, in that comparatively small world, knowing about the Savior.

Does loving this way come naturally for those who trust Christ? It begins with trusting Him, but it is enhanced by other exercises. It is necessary to get near people before we can love them. A member of the younger set was reprimanding her parents for spending so much time with soap operas and said she did not see how they could stand them. Her dad's response was, "But you don't know these people like we do." It is necessary to know real-life people and to be quite aware of their needs, which remind us of where they are without Christ, before we will love them like we must.

It is also in order to pray for the necessary love. That's what Paul did for the Philippian Christians. "My prayer for you is that you will overflow more and more with love for others" (Phil. 1:9a, TLB).

Evidently the prayer was impressively answered, for the church at Philippi seemed to be one of the most effective early segments of believers.

III. A Willingness to Pay a Price

Someone said, "There is no bargain day in the kingdom of God." Jesus made this fact very clear. He told of a man who sold all he had in order to buy the treasure which he found hid in a field. He told a wealthy young inquirer that the way to eternal life was to sell all that he had. He reminded another would-be follower that if he went with Him, he would be following Someone who had no place to lay His head.

Wherever a body of believers which is alive, which has a contagious faith, from which light shines into a dark world, is found, somebody is paying a price. Hear the apostle cry out, "Now I have given up everything else" (Phil. 3:10a, TLB).

It is dependent upon what we want to be as a church. It is decided at the point of how important we think our mission is in the year before us. It hinges on how urgent a matter it is to us. A crowd who will settle for nothing less than being a pocket of spiritual prosperity will pay the price.

26

IV. A Confidence that God Will Provide the Resources

David Livingstone returned to his alma mater, Glasgow University, after 18 years in Africa, to receive an honorary degree. In keeping with a traditional practice, a group of hecklers had planned to detract from the ceremony. The story goes, however, that when Livingstone appeared at the rostrum, gaunt, wrinkled by 27 fevers, darkened by the sun, with one arm hanging limp due to a lion's bite, he presented a spectacle which awed and quieted the assembly. Among other things, he said, "I am going back. Shall I tell you what sustained me amidst the toil, hardship, and loneliness of my exiled life? It was the promise, 'Lo, I am with you alway, even unto the end' " (Matt. 28:20b).

To his petition for relief from affliction Paul got this tremendous word of assurance: "But my God shall supply all your need according to his riches in glory by Christ Jesus" (Phil. 4:19). That's a sustaining word, too.

A pocket of spiritual prosperity—a likely description for a body of believers ready to be the church our world needs in the new year.

H. B. LONDON, Jr., is pastor of the First Church of the Nazarene of Salem, Ore., where he has served since 1968. He is a graduate of Pasadena College and Nazarene Theological Seminary, and has also received the Litt.D. degree from the California Graduate School of Theology. His previous pastorates were in Whittier and Bloomington, Calif.

Under his leadership Salem First has experienced marked and continued growth in all areas. The congregation has given outstanding support to world mission programs, and Work and Witness teams from the church have ministered in mission areas around the world.

Rev. London is a frequent speaker at retreats and conferences, and, in addition to his pastoral ministry, speaks on a daily radio program and a weekly television program. He has served the denomination as a district youth president, District Church Schools chairman, District Advisory Board member, and is currently serving on the Board of Trustees of Nazarene Bible College.

HOLY WEEK

H. B. London, Jr.

When I consider the subjects of Good Friday, Palm Sunday, and those events surrounding the Easter Day, such as the encounter Jesus had with the men on the road to Emmaus, I am reminded of God's love for me through His Son, Jesus Christ. It is because of that love for me that I must share these beautiful events with those to whom I have been called to minister.

I shall not forget my experience in Jerusalem: the busy streets, the noise, the smells; then the quiet—of a garden in Gethsemane, the tomb, the unbelievably dark nights.

There are those memories of days gone by: Jesus Christ praying for His disciples; the Master moving in regal splendor through the streets of the Holy City; God's Son suffering the pain, the humiliation of a shameful execution. I can almost hear the sobs of my Savior who loved His children so very much; the shouts of acclaim by those who knew there was something very special about Jesus, but did not know for sure what it was; the wailing of those who stood by and watched Him suffer—and die.

I like to share with those who will listen, my impression of the unforgettable days of triumph and agony—those moments of ecstasy and torment. I endeavor to paint a picture, to unfold a canvas that will in some way transport my audience back in time, to a time nearly 2,000 years ago that was lawless and pagan. It was a time when it was very unpopular to be a follower of the carpenter's Son from

Galilee, a time where being a Christian really cost something, where faith was as important to one's day as food and drink. It was a day where the badge of Christian discipleship was not a lapel pin, an identity chain around one's neck, or a bumper sticker. The badge of Christian discipleship was rather a life-style, a love, a commitment to a cause and a creed.

It is through the use of the special days like Palm Sunday, Good Friday, and other days surrounding the death and resurrection of Jesus Christ that I am able to focus on the very important themes of discipleship, loyalty, and commitment.

There is an urgent call in this day for a once-and-for-all loyalty to the mission of Christ, a never-say-die commitment to His person and message. Because we live in a day of fickle followers, fair-weather worshipers, and slumbering saints, it is so very vital that we take advantage of special days to draw attention to the fact that it is not easy to be a Christian; it never has been, and it never will be. Because of this, we need a renewed commitment on the part of those who call Jesus Lord, to stand up and be counted—regardless of the cost.

Palm Sunday—A 2,000-Year Echo

SCRIPTURE: Luke 19:28-44; Matt. 26:69-75

In March of 1980, I had the opportunity to speak to a group of Christians in a small town in western India. There were approximately 75 people jammed into a small living room of an Indian home. I read to them from Matthew, chapter 26—the story of Peter and his denial of Jesus. In his denial he declared, "I don't know anything about the man."

I challenged those Christians to be faithful to the One they called their Savior. As I spoke to them, I was reminded that it would not be so easy to be a Christian in a country of 700 million people that was way over 90 percent something else; not so easy to turn one's back on pagan religions when they were the going thing; not so easy to bow the knee at the foot of Jesus Christ and proclaim Him Lord when very few others did.

I told that brave group of Christians, "You must never be ashamed of Christ; you must never give up your faith; you must never be afraid." My authority for saying these things to this persecuted group of believers came from the words of Jesus when He declared, "Whoever acknowledges me before men, I will also acknowledge him before my Father in heaven. But whoever disowns me before men, I will disown him before my Father in heaven" (Matt. 10: 32-33, NIV). He spoke these words to a group of people who were grossly outnumbered, who were afraid and uncertain of their faith, and who had little hope except through their faith.

Today, nearly 2,000 years later, the echo of the words of Jesus Christ still sound loudly to all who would stop to listen: *Be faithful!*

I. The Palm Sunday Story (Luke 19:28-44)

Jesus spent His last Sabbath in Bethany with His friends. The news had already begun to circulate that He was coming into Jerusalem. The Bible narrative reports that as He approached the city, a great multitude came to meet Him. Among them were not only the citizens of Jerusalem, but also those who had come up for the Feast of the Passover, and, of course, the Pharisees who hated Him so. Also present were the Roman authorities who had been put on alert during the great feast times lest there be some kind of revolution.

31

It is interesting to note that on all other occasions Jesus Christ had rejected the false enthusiasm of the people. He had fled the spotlight of publicity (Matt. 16:20; Mark 5:43; 9:9; John 7:6).

Now, the time had come, and there was acclaim. Garments lined the road before Him; limbs from olive trees were strewn along the way. And the shouts of recognition were deafening; they cried, "Blessings on him who comes as king in the name of the Lord" (Luke 19:38, NEB).

Jesus openly admitted now that He was the One sent from God. To those who would seek to quiet His subjects along the way, His response was one of awful majesty. He responded, "I tell you, if my disciples keep silence the stones will shout aloud" (v. 40, NEB).

Yet, amidst all the pomp and ceremony there was sadness in the heart of Jesus Christ. Though He was King, and though they recognized Him as King, He knew that the welcome would be fleeting. He looked at the city and He cried, saying, "If only you had known, on this great day, the way that leads to peace! But no; it is hidden from your sight" (v. 42, NEB).

II. The Palm Sunday Stain (Matt. 26:69-75)

The parade is over now; the palm branches have all been swept up and the clothes gathered by those who threw them. Jesus had been taken before the authorities. The scene turns to a man by the name of Peter; and in six words that epitomize him and the world in which we live, he said, "I do not know the man" (Matt. 26:74, NEB). These words were spoken by a man who all of a sudden was ashamed of the best thing that had ever come into his life.

This can happen. You may think it won't, but it happens. It happens to the best of us in those moments when we are called upon to make some obvious stand. We somehow forget that at one time we were shouting hosannas and spreading palm branches in the path of the Son of God. It happens because of fatigue, peer pressure, and unfulfilled willingness to follow the will of God; perhaps by a selfish desire to run things our own way. Who knows? But when it happens, the same sense of sorrow that caused Jesus to cry as He overlooked the city of Jerusalem, causes Him to cry anew. That pain of rejection echoes down through the channels of time—2,000 years later.

III. The Palm Sunday Affirmation

If we know anything about the Christian religion, we know that from its beginning it has been spread largely by those of us who would share our faith in Christ. It was to Peter, Andrew, and the disciples that Jesus said, "Follow me, and I will make you fishers of men" (Matt. 4:19). The echo of those words continues today, much as the words did 2,000 years ago. Jesus Christ continues to lay down the same call before all who will become His disciples.

When we follow, He asks us to: (1) Make our faith real to others. We cannot give away something we do not have; but when we have genuinely believed, we begin our pilgrimage as a Christian disciple. (2) Witness to our faith. Technically, we know that a witness is someone who is present when something of significance happens. When we express this dynamic faith, it does two things: *(a)* It fortifies the person who gives the witness; *(b)* it moves the ordinary hearer of the witness to acknowledge their own need.

You hold the key to eternal life! Not just for yourself but for many. You must be so convinced of your faith and in your ability that, even though all others remain silent, you will continue to proclaim Jesus Christ as Lord. The hosannas, the palm branches, the show of deep appreciation

—these must flow from your life even in an hour when other men grow strangely silent.

When Jesus entered Jerusalem, He cried, because He knew that men would eventually reject the opportunity to receive Him. In disobeying Him, they would destroy themselves. By denying Him, they denied the Central Figure of all history, their only hope—the Son of God, who rode into their world to give them life abundant and everlasting.

Ask yourself some questions: "On this Palm Sunday, how loyal are you to Christ? How convinced are you of the truth of His message? How committed are you to the mission He represents? How courageous are you in sharing your faith?"

The echo of Palm Sunday will continue just as long as you continue to raise your voice and your faith in honor of the King of Kings and Lord of Lords.

Coronation with Concern

SCRIPTURE: Luke 19:38-42

The Palm Sunday parade was merely the culmination of a long procession that had started three years before. One day Jesus told His disciples, "We go up to Jerusalem, and all things that are written by the prophets concerning [Me] shall be accomplished" (Luke 18:31).

It was following this statement that the real Palm Sunday parade began. It was on this journey that Jesus met and ministered to those He had found along the way. It was the beginning of a journey that would change the course of history.

I. Prelude to the Parade

Luke tells us of three situations that underscore the ministry of Jesus Christ as He made His way to Jerusalem.

A. *Jesus Met Blind Bartimaeus.* The blind man stepped out from the crowd and cried, "Jesus, . . . have mercy on me" (Luke 18:38; cf. Mark 10:46). It was as Jesus ministered to the blind beggar that He showed His concern over the physical needs of all mankind. Many who suffer from physical ailments and infirmities could be healed just as Bartimaeus if they were willing to step out of the crowd and call upon the healing powers of the Son of God.

B. *Jesus Met Zaccheus.* It was in Jericho on His way to Jerusalem that Jesus met the little tax collector. It was from this encounter that Zaccheus responded to the life-changing invitation of Jesus Christ. In response to the little man's acceptance of Jesus as God's Son, He said of him, "Today salvation has come to this house" (Luke 19:9, NIV). Along the way to Jerusalem, Jesus was very concerned about the spiritual needs of mankind.

C. *Jesus Taught a Lesson.* Another very interesting thing happened along the way to Jerusalem. Jesus had the opportunity to teach the people a very important lesson. It was the simple story of a rich man who had gone away on a trip, leaving his servants to handle an investment. When he returned, he required of them that which he had given, plus the interest earned. Two of them had handled the money well, but one, because of fear, had failed to invest the treasure wisely. Thus, through the parable Jesus expressed the truth that the one who invests his life and talent wisely for the Lord will be given even greater treasure than he had ever thought possible (Luke 19:26).

On His way to Jerusalem, Jesus ministered to the total needs of mankind. His prelude to Palm Sunday was to recognize the needs of all mankind and minister to them.

II. Coronation by the Curious

I walked the supposed route of that Palm Sunday parade much like I would walk the Rose Parade route after a New Year's Day celebration—the music of the bands still very fresh in the mind, the joy of the experience still flooding the heart.

The day I walked where Jesus walked, it was bright and clear; and in my mind's eye I pictured the Palm Sunday parade. I could see the Central Figure, Jesus Christ, seated regally upon the donkey. It was obvious to see that He loved His people very much; and as they thronged around Him that day, I would notice they were common people for the most part. They loved Him, and they wanted to make Him a king. He had healed their sick, opened their eyes, restored to them their hearing. He had delivered them from fear, had helped to ease away their pain. They had feelings that demanded to be expressed, and on this day Jesus Christ would not deny them that right.

Had I been in the crowd Palm Sunday, I would have wanted to be heard. I would have waved a branch or two and shed my coat that Jesus Christ might feel even more majestic. For He has done so much for me; how could I remain silent?

Yet the day was a coronation by the curious. For as I walked the parade route into Jerusalem, I could not only sense the excitement of the sincere, but I could also feel the antagonism, the jealousy, the misunderstanding, the fickle attitude of many. The faith of the curious would wither even before the olive branches hit the ground; and when the vote was taken, when Pilate would cry out, "And who will be for Christ?" the voices of the curious would be strangely silent. In this, the 20th century, as I walked where Jesus walked, one fact was most sobering—that the multitude who loved Him so on the day of the parade were strangely silent on the day of the trial.

III. A King Responds to the Coronation

As Jerusalem burst into view, the Bible says that when Jesus "saw the city, he wept over it" (Luke 19:41, NIV). Others might have seen the city for gain, for pleasure, for power; but Jesus saw in it a people who were heading helplessly for the judgment. If they had only responded; if they had only recognized that Jesus was more than just a man—that He was a Savior; if they had only responded to the choices they had been given, things might have been so different.

History has not changed us. Jesus Christ walks into our lives; He draws near; and how we respond to His appearing is so very important. Jesus said then, and He says now, "Here I am! I stand at the door and knock. If anyone hears my voice and opens the door, I will go in and eat with him, and he with me" (Rev. 3:20, NIV). The Word of God advises all men, "Today if you hear His voice, do not harden your hearts" (Heb. 3:7-8, NASB); "Now is 'the acceptable time,' behold, now is 'the day of salvation'" (2 Cor. 6:2, NASB).

It may be that He is growing near to you today and that He has been making His presence felt for some time now. The awesome confrontation of being where Christ is calls each of us to make a decision. Will we proclaim Him as Lord, or will we deny Him as just another king?

When I walked one day where Jesus walked, I could imagine the throng of people who had loved Him very much. I could feel the presence of those who refused His offer, His love, His overture of peace. I could feel the heartbeat of the King.

Conclusion

Crowds, noise, palm branches—all turned to silence. They had been called upon to make a commitment to the

Carpenter King. At the heart and at the center of the message of Jesus Christ is that gentle calling for men to recognize Him for what He is. There is nothing more important than pausing in your walk along life's road to realize that He is meant to be your Savior and Lord. It is the moment of truth where you pause in your pursuit for personal satisfaction to bow your knee at the feet of Jesus Christ and proclaim Him King. Recognize Him for what He is—Healer, Miracle Man, Teacher, but most of all, the Savior of all men, who died on the Cross that you might have life abundant and everlasting.

As I walked one day where Jesus walked, I was assured that He had become royalty for me. He wore the crown of concern that cost Him His life. I would be less than grateful if I did not join that throng along the parade route in singing, "Rejoice . . . shout . . . behold, thy King cometh" (Zech. 9:9).

I walked one day where Jesus walked, and I felt His presence there.

Three Lights for a Dark Day

(Good Friday)

SCRIPTURE: Luke 22:46; 23:42; John 19:30

There are many things that happen to us; and at first glance or notice, they seem to be disastrous. Yet, we have lived long enough to realize that many things are blessings in disguise. For example, we miss an airplane and find out later in the news that the plane has crashed. What was sorrow becomes victory. We go in for a physical checkup, and the doctor discovers something that calls for an operation. The news of surgery scares us, but the result of the surgery is that life will no longer be in danger.

Good Friday was one of those days—a black, gloomy day, but one that was a prelude to the sunshine of Easter. It was a day that had to be. It was an event that could not be disregarded.

We would like to highlight three isolated events that surrounded Good Friday. First, we will look at the Garden of Gethsemane, where Jesus was praying with His disciples. Let us call this a moment of rebuke. Then we will turn to an event of the Cross—the moment that concerned one who was guilty of sin against God and his fellowman. We will call this event a call for restitution. The final event of our Good Friday message will concern one of the seven last words of Jesus: "It is finished." This we will call a time for recognition.

I. A Moment of Rebuke (Luke 22:46)

Jesus had gone out into the Mount of Olives to pray. When He reached the place, He told the disciples, "Pray that you will not fall into temptation." He then went a stone's throw beyond them and began to pray himself. He prayed, "Father, if you are willing, take this cup from me; yet not my will, but yours be done" (Luke 22:40, 42, NIV).

When He returned from this prayer, He found that His disciples were asleep. He rebuked them: "Get up and pray so that you will not fall into temptation" (v. 46, NIV). Jesus knew what was ahead of them. He could not explain it in such a way that they would understand, yet He knew. He knew that they would suffer untold persecution. He knew that they would be faced with challenges beyond their wildest expectations. He knew that in just a few hours their faith would be tested to the breaking point. He knew they needed strength from His Heavenly Father.

When Christ cried out, "Let this cup pass from me" (Matt. 26:39), He was not shrinking from the Cross. But the Cross contained the bitterness of His mortal pain, the loneliness of shame, and mental anguish. It was a curse that was to be endured by Him and no other. It was a lonely cross. His disciples whom He had chosen were already beginning to leave Him. They were afraid.

When you consider the disciples' plight, you must remember your times of loneliness—the depression, rejection, and uncertainty you have faced. We all need the assurance that we will never go through our Gethsemanes alone.

Gethsemane is only a little grove of olive trees on the slope of a mountain across the valley from Jerusalem. Yet, it remains a symbol of agony and loneliness, a symbol of man's inability to be all that man needs to be. When Jesus needed His friends the most, they were asleep.

I am reminded on this Good Friday that never will I struggle through a Gethsemane of my own alone. Jesus is conscious of my need. Jesus did not rebuke His followers because of His loneliness, but because He knew they would need the strength that His Father would have given them through prayer; thus the rebuke.

II. A Call for Restitution (Luke 23:42)

Good Friday was a black day; the clouds were heavy and the silence was almost breathtaking. Jesus was hanging now between two thieves. They were convicted criminals. They had listened to Jesus speak from the Cross, and one of them had grown very curious.

It was a beautiful moment in an otherwise tragic scene. A convicted criminal, while being executed, had a moment to examine his own life. In Jesus Christ he saw One who caused his life to look very empty. He stopped trying to rationalize his own plight and noted something very important was missing. He found in Jesus Christ a light for a better tomorrow, where a few moments before, the black wall had loomed so high. It was on this bleak day on Calvary that a hardened sinner turned from his own self to Jesus Christ.

He prayed. He didn't pray to God as we might imagine, for he had seen so much of God in the One beside him that he offered to Christ a prayer. At a time when the mobs were hurling insults to the dying Man, he was praying to Him. He did not pray for anything else except for himself. He prayed for mercy.

In the bleakness of a desperate day he saw a throne, not a Cross; a glorious King, not a suffering Savior. He implored, "Remember me." And Jesus, responding to the sincerity of the one beside Him, responded, "Today shalt thou be with me [and forevermore]" (Luke 23:43).

Today, Good Friday, the truth of God's Word comes ringing true: Nothing can separate us from the love of God (Rom. 8:35, 37). Not heartbreak, sorrow, rejection—not even death. Because of Christ, through the love of God, we are remembered and rewarded; we are forgiven.

III. A Time for Recognition (John 19:30)

Jesus cried from the Cross, "It is finished." In so doing, He was declaring, "My earthly ministry is completed." He had finished the task His Father had given Him (17:4). He was also saying that His redemptive ministry was finished. He had come as a Savior to all mankind, and now the price for the world's sin had been paid. The Cross became His workshop from which He stripped the forces of hell of all their authority.

Where humanity is often overshadowed by the tragic sense of the incomplete; where many men start with good intentions to build towers and find it impossible to finish, Jesus Christ had completed the job He had been called to complete.

A. *His words* called for recognition—they still do!

1. His enemies thought His words would forever still the claims He had made.

2. His friends thought His words meant the recognition of a life completed. He would be at rest now. And this was some consolation.

3. His Heavenly Father recognized that His Son would no longer be faced with human limitations. Now, the burden of sin He had carried for so long was lifted. The blood that He shed would prove to all that there was hope. The price had been paid. Jesus Christ had finished His ministry, His redemptive work; man need never walk in darkness again.

Conclusion

To the world, Good Friday was a black day of pain and agony, a day filled with injustice and bitterness. Yet, when I look at Good Friday, I see a light that will follow men down the channels of time to this very day.

We need to be rebuked for our sleepy faithlessness.

We need to humble ourselves before the Master and ask for His forgiveness.

And praise be to God, we can recognize Him today as a living, loving Lord.

Like many things in life, Good Friday was a blessing in disguise. Because Christ died (His Father turned sunlight into darkness, then vice versa on Easter morning), He was given the opportunity to live. Because He lives, we shall live—forever.

Walking to Emmaus

SCRIPTURE: Luke 24:13-35

TEXT: *And we had hoped that he would be the one* (Luke 24:21, TEV).

(NOTE: In my ministry I have always given the Sunday following Easter to a message on the Emmaus Road. I have done it for the purpose of encouraging those who have been hurt, disappointed, and disillusioned at life. I have done it to encourage them to keep their eyes and their lives open to the presence of Jesus Christ. To those of us who accept Him as the resurrected Lord, He will always be that Presence beside us wherever we go or in whatever situations we have been asked to endure.)

Malcolm Muggeridge, once an atheist, was sent by the BBC to Palestine to film a television documentary on the life of Christ. The more he involved himself in the filming of the documentary, the more interested he became in the fact of the Resurrection. It seemed to make sense. In the final episode, he walked along the Emmaus Road in an attempt to catch the spirit of those two followers of Christ on that first Easter morning; he then expressed his faith in God. He declared, "I am assured of this point, that there is always a presence ready to emerge from the shadows and to fall in step along the dusty, stoney way, regardless of what you may have been asked to endure."

The presence of Christ is always recognizable if we open up our lives to Him.

Cleopas and his friend had left the Holy City completely defeated. But like Malcolm Muggeridge, the result of their journey to Emmaus was life changing. Something happened—their unbelief fell by the wayside and was replaced by a tiny spark of faith. Muggeridge recounted that, like the two, he returned to Jerusalem, saying, "The

Lord is risen indeed . . . Did not our heart burn within us, while he talked with us by the way?" (Luke 24:34, 32). It is in times of loss, heartbreak, and rejection that we can feel the divine presence of our Lord Jesus Christ.

I. Where Is Emmaus?

Emmaus is a place you go when somebody you love very much has just passed away. Emmaus is a place you go to get away from it all when things have not gone the way you had planned. Emmaus is a place where you go in retreat to try and figure out the backhand slaps of life.

In reality, Emmaus is a seven-mile walk from Jerusalem. But for people like you and me, Emmaus is retreat.

On that Easter morning, most of the followers of Christ had gone in one way or another to Emmaus. The disillusioned Peter and the other disciples were at loose ends. Nobody knew for sure where Thomas was. But Emmaus for the followers of Christ was a place to go, to get away!

Emmaus is a place where all of us go when the world has pretty well crashed around us—a place to hide out, to escape, to regroup. Emmaus is where we go when it seems our resources never materialized. Emmaus is escape—but to what? The road to Emmaus is littered with so many drug addicts and alcoholics. Emmaus has been the scene of much immorality or a simple surrender to a lesser life. Emmaus for many has been the route to the second best. It is for some a cop-out. To others, "What's the use?" or, "Who cares?"

Emmaus is where we go when we have great doubts and fears, when life did not play by the rules. Emmaus is where we go when we feel we have been shortchanged, when the knot at the end of the rope fails to hold. Emmaus is where the followers of Jesus went to try and forget about Him and their disappointments. Emmaus is where we go when our hearts are just about to break.

44

II. The Road to Emmaus Is No Escape

The fact that you go to Emmaus to get away from it all does not mean that you will succeed. Cleopas and his friend were going to Emmaus in retreat, but the Bible says, "Later that day he appeared to two who were walking from Jerusalem into the country, but they didn't recognize him at first because he had changed his appearance" (Mark 16:12, TLB).

You may think that you are alone on your retreat, but in reality you are not and never can be.

It is precisely at this time—on the road away from things that bother us, the things that seem to be our undoing—that the question is asked by One who loves us more than any other, "The road you are traveling, My friend—where will it take you? What is the real reason for your trip to Emmaus?"

What happens when we stop to consider this question? He comes in a marvelous fashion. Jesus himself, the resurrected Lord, comes with the offer of help and love. He promises never to leave us. He promises us strength sufficient. He promises us grace to overcome any temptation. He promises us guidance for the dark moments of life. Jesus walks into our midst alive, real, and full of love and concern for the situation we face.

III. Finding a Friend on the Way to Emmaus

We bury ourselves in the record of the past. Jesus cannot be contained there—in the past. We only recognize Him as we live with Him through the realities of everyday life—here and now! When you stop and think about it, even the disciples failed to recognize Christ when He appeared. Mary mistook Him for a gardener. Cleopas and his friend failed to recognize Him even though they walked with Him. Somehow after the bottom has dropped out of everything, we really don't expect Him to be walking our way.

Many days after the Resurrection Peter was fishing. He didn't recognize Jesus standing on the beach simply because Peter assumed that Christ would not be interested in him anymore. What a terrible assumption! Yet this is so like us; when we have been disappointed and when our lives seem to be on unsteady footing, we have a tendency to think, Who cares? The answer is, God cares!

It is at this point that Jesus Christ calls you by name, encouraging you: "Recognize Me; you are a fortunate person." And you are! Fortunate because life has pushed you to the end of yourself. Fortunate because you have come to a place where you realize that you just can't cope alone anymore. A place where your only alternative is to throw yourself upon God for safety and healing. In times like this our eyes are opened to a point of recognition. We recognize it is Jesus and Jesus only who can minister to the deepest needs of our lives.

The whole world may look like winter to you today. When you started out for Emmaus, you were getting away from it all. But you see, they laid Him in a grave, and God raised Him; now the sun is out and there is life in the air. There is blue sky, soft breezes, and warm sunshine.

Jesus said to those travelers on the Emmaus Road what He says to you. Look back if you want to. See Good Friday, but don't live there, for the record speaks most about the Resurrection. Move on from seeing just the pain and the heartbreak, and remember that there is springtime. Jesus is urging, "Recognize Me for who I am. I am truly the resurrected Lord." (See John 11:25.)

Conclusion

Are you on your way to Emmaus today? Away from disappointments, burdened down with cares and problems? Are you on your way to Emmaus, refusing to really face the facts as they are—you are in trouble and you need help? Are you on your way to Emmaus today, fighting overwhelming odds, when you really don't have to? If you will allow Him, Jesus Christ will appear, He will take your hand, and He will guide you back to Jerusalem.

No, going to Emmaus is not bad. In fact, it might be the most important journey of your life, if in going to Emmaus you are helped to recognize Jesus Christ.

RUSSELL METCALFE is pastor of the Wollaston Church of the Nazarene on the campus of Eastern Nazarene College in Quincy, Mass. A pastor for 25 years, 13 of which were spent in the metropolitan New York City area, Pastor Metcalfe has been college pastor in his present assignment since 1977.

He is a frequent contributor to Nazarene periodicals and is the author of *The Beauty of Holiness,* published by the Nazarene Publishing House.

EASTER

Russell Metcalfe

Ideally, three elements come into an effective focus in the preaching of every sermon. These elements are: (1) the personality and spiritual preparation of the preacher; (2) the gathering, selection, and application of the scriptural material that is preached; and (3) the effectiveness of the actual delivery of the sermon. And while the three elements cannot be separated, still each of the three must be given careful and deliberate attention.

Often the preparation of the preacher for preaching is not considered an integral part of sermon preparation. Fitness for the pulpit may be the unconscious by-product of a viable, healthy prayer life. Certainly, a minister who habitually, for his own soul's sake, spends time alone with God cannot help at the same time to be preparing himself to stand as God's man before his congregation.

Yet it needs to be recognized and stated: The preparation of the person who preaches is the most important part of the sermon! And during seasonal emphases of the church year this personal spiritual preparation for preaching becomes even more important, if possible, than usual. For unless the "old, old story" has a fresh, fresh grasp on the preacher, even the profound truths of the Incarnation, the Atonement, the Resurrection, and heart holiness will sound forth the tinny notes of shibboleth.

My personal preparation for Easter preaching always meets the usual complications and obstacles of a parish and community in pre-holiday activity. There is a general excitement in the days preceding Easter that does not always enhance meditation on the deep spiritual truth we would proclaim. And so, in a nonliturgical way, I always make my people aware that I, personally, will be trying to prepare my own soul for a fresh appreciation of Christ's great victory by retracing Christ's passion during the Lenten season. There can be no real awareness of the magnitude of the Resurrection apart from looking again and again at our Savior's *kenosis*, and apart from a willingness to share in His sufferings.

Also I reread such books as J. Glenn Gould's *Precious Blood of Christ,* and authors such as Purkiser, R. Taylor, W. Taylor, and Wiley—those sections that deal with the death and resurrection of Christ. As I read, I am deeply aware of current needs in my congregation; and I meditate on just how Christ's victory over sin, death, and hell speaks to these very real family situations.

I ask God to help me keep the main focus of the worship of the church on the preached Word, while at the same time not slighting the music and the children's emphases as of little or no importance. In short, I make a deliberate attempt to prepare myself for Easter.

The content of the Easter sermon need not be limited to the narratives that deal directly with Resurrection Day, although every pastor should share with his congregation at some time or other the breathless boldness of Peter as he brushes past his younger companion to burst into the empty tomb. Every pastor should tell again and again the story of how Mary could not recognize her risen Lord until He spoke her name; and every congregation should hear over and over the unanswerable question of the angel: "Why seek ye the living among the dead?" (Luke 24:5).

And yet Resurrection power permeates the entire Book! Christ's mastery of death is tangent to every human need and can be seen in every facet of divine revelation. If the pastor is in a series of sermons in some book of the Bible other than a Gospel or Pauline epistle, it may well be that without any wresting whatsoever, the passage that would naturally fall to the Easter date would give unique insight into truth about the power of Christ's life that meets perfectly both the demands of the calendar and the needs of the congregation. The truth is there, relevant, waiting appropriation and application by the faithful pastor.

I include examples of different kinds of Easter sermons: implicit Easter truth from a passage not directly dealing with the Resurrection story; traditional narrative; topical application of a text; textual.

The Book, the Lamb, and the Song

TEXT: Rev. 5:9-14

Introduction

Easter, of all days, should be a time of praise to Jesus Christ for His mighty victory over sin and death in our behalf. Such praise is a dominant theme in heaven. Nowhere in all Scripture is a more magnificent hymn than John's "Worthy Is the Lamb." (I am certain heaven has better tunes; but until I get there, Handel's will do!)

From the content of John's hymn of praise (text) comes the thought I would share with you this Resurrection Day, as well as praise in which I would have us join at the close. For in this chapter John tells us of a mysterious *book*, and of a mighty *Lamb*, and of a magnificent *song*.

I. The Book That Was Sealed

A. The sight of the unopened book caused John to weep.

   1. Some "books in God's library" include: all the deeds of personal human history; all the demands of God's laws; all the experience of God's beloved; all the names of those redeemed by the Blood (Ps. 69:28; Gal. 3:10; Mal. 3:16; Phil. 4:3).

   2. Some "books" that bring us sorrow:
      a. sorrow of unresolved inequities
      b. sorrow of unknown, fearful future
      c. sorrow of uncertain salvation

B. John's sorrow is all mankind's sorrow. Apart from the Lamb and the song there is sorrow; and even the Bible itself is a sealed book apart from Jesus! But John's story does not end with weeping.

II. The Lamb That Was Slain

A. "Weep not!" An elder lifts John's vision. There is a strange mixture of figures here. "Behold the *Lion!*" Lion, Lamb, Root, Judah! (See v. 5, NIV.) Slain in innocence, meekness, and patience, now Christ is seen as mighty and powerful, striking terror to the hearts of His enemies while at the same time bringing comfort to His people. ("Of Judah" means this is no "spiritual resurrection"; Christ is One *with us!*)

B. One feature of the Lamb stands out above others: *It has been slain!* At the throne, identified with God himself, it yet bears the marks of having died! *The heart of Easter truth is very near this point!*

C. The *Lamb*—identified as "of Judah" and yet having the seven eyes and seven horns of the sevenfold Spirit of God—is *able* to open the sealed book!

III. The Song That Was Sung

(Indeed, this song *is* being sung today and will *always* be sung!)

A. The song is *begun* by the redeemed (v. 9). The new song is a song of *redemption*. And while the angels are quick to join in praise, they do not have part in the very first chorus, for the heart of Easter is *not* the return of springtime, the eternal conservation of life, or the beauty of flowers and birdsong. The heart of Easter is the *fact* of bloody battle and stunning victory, of alienated mankind brought into fellowship with a holy God, and at the very foot of the throne becoming a great *family* that includes every tongue, people, and nation (v. 9).

B. The song, picked up by heaven's chorus, *praises* the Lamb because He alone is worthy to open the sealed book. Christ is our key to the mysteries of faith—of death, eternity, and redemption.

C. The song is actually begun *before* the books are opened. We may praise Jesus now; and even before we know the future, we may know Him with certainty!

D. And we may begin *now*, joining the myriads around the throne as we sing: "Crown Him . . . the Lamb upon the throne!"

Conclusion

But before we sing a hymn of praise to Christ, are there *sealed books* that cause you to weep? Is the *Bible* a sealed book to you? Do you have deep concern about *death* and about the *future*?

The word to John is the word to us all:

"Weep not!"

The message of Easter is: The Lion of the tribe of Judah *has prevailed!*

The Stone Rolled Away

TEXT: *And they found the stone rolled away* (Luke 24:2).

Introduction

Mark tells us the women were worrying as they came near the graveyard, for the stone was large, and they did not know how it could ever be moved. (Two things are wonderful about this story: (1) the honesty of the Scriptures, as they show just how slowly the disciples were to grasp the truth of the Resurrection; and (2) the love and loyalty to Jesus that these people had, even though in their minds He was dead.) But these loving "unbelievers" never had to finish their mission.

The stone was rolled away, and the nature of their mission of love for Jesus was dramatically changed. The power of the Resurrection removed those things which block our faith:

I. The Stone of Anguish Was Replaced with a Growing Peace

A. This peace was not necessarily a once-for-all-time removal of difficulty. But when they realized that Jesus had not died a martyr's death—what a difference!

B. Jesus had promised: "My peace I give unto you" (John 14:27). Now they began to understand.

II. The Stone of Empty, Disappointed Faith Gave Way to Certainty

A. Of all days of the year, on Easter I am most thankful to be a simple gospel preacher. If I did not literally believe that Jesus lives, what would I have to say?

B. The stone was not removed to let Jesus out, but to permit us to see *in!* It was a literal, bodily resurrection.

C. Humanism's "fact" sounds brave and suave and wise; but it is empty! Talking of resurrection in terms of "Christian observance of springtime" is really to turn things inside out. The miracle of springtime is mute testimony to the greater miracle of life—the eternal life that is our Savior's resurrection!

D. This comes to me with special impact as I stand beside the open grave. [Here I mention the saints who have died the past year.] Those who die in Christ shall certainly, literally, rise again! "In my flesh shall I see God!"

III. The Stone of Dead Scripture (Heavy Laws to Fulfill) Is Gone, Replaced by the Illumination of the Word by the Risen Savior

A. The walk to Emmaus—Jesus opened the Scriptures (Luke 24:13-35).

B. One certain sign that the power of the Resurrection is at work in you is the craving of your heart and mind for the Bible.

C. The Scriptures really do not make sense apart from this Day of Resurrection. All truth begins to glow as it centers in this one great fact.

IV. The Stone of "Religion" Becomes a Living Relationship with God That Sustains

A. Isaiah's taunt (Isa. 46:1-4) about Babylon's gods that must be carried about, while Jehovah God bears His people lovingly.

B. . . . is exactly what Paul speaks of as worthy of any sacrifice, the dynamic that transforms all of life (Phil. 3: 10): "the power of his resurrection"!

Conclusion

Jesus wants to release this mighty Resurrection power in us!

Is there a great stone in your life? anguish that you struggle with? a disappointment? or a striving to keep the law? a faith that somehow doesn't work? (A father who makes his home a hell on earth? A teenager who wishes that he could be himself, and still really be Christ's? An older person who is lonely and feeling absolutely abandoned?)

These are stones that can be removed! It is not a simple thing, and yet it begins when we do not just accept other peoples' word for it—that Jesus is alive. It begins when we want to find out for ourselves!

Is He really *risen?* Can He really meet with *me?* Will you come with me to the empty tomb—and see?

Walk to Emmaus

Text: Luke 24:13-35; 2 Cor. 5:16-17

Introduction

It seems that Paul had a problem. There were people in the church at Corinth who were saying to Paul: "*You* never knew Jesus in the flesh; but *we* did!" These people "knew" Jesus but didn't really *know* Him. But Paul retorts, "No! Even if we did know Jesus after the flesh, that is not the way we know Him now." Jesus must be spiritually revealed and discerned by obedient *faith*.

Whether with Mary in the Garden, by the seaside, in the closed room, or here on the Emmaus walk, "Old things were passed away; . . . all things had become new." (See 2 Cor. 5:16-17.) Especially the way Jesus revealed himself to them—and reveals himself to us!

Look at this one example of how Jesus was spiritually revealed (from Luke 24):

I. The Disciples Were:

A. *Sad* (v. 17). There is no lasting joy apart from living hope, apart from God and His Son.

B. *Discouraged* (v. 21). "We *trusted*." (But we don't trust anymore!) Faith in the past tense; hope gone.

C. *Unbelieving* (v. 25). Folly—and worse! They were "slow of heart to believe," but they were gently rebuked. Their sinful nature could not unaided grasp spiritual truth.

II. The Savior Was:

A. *A Companion in their walk* (even before they knew it, v. 15). (Did you ever have Jesus "slip up beside you" when you were not really expecting Him, but when you needed Him very much? It is possible that Jesus is near at hand and ready to break into our consciousness more often than we realize!)

B. *An Expositor of the Scriptures* (v. 27). Jesus always brings us knowledge of himself and of salvation along the avenue of the Scriptures.

1. Not until the Bible is opened do we see our sin and unbelief as the root of the problem.

2. Not until we see the truth from Him do we see that the ultimate sin is just that—*unbelief*.

3. Jesus revealed himself, finally, as a *friend*. The dominant thing, and the thing that had continuity with the Jesus they remembered, was *love*. (And what pastor would

not give all the books in his library to have heard that exposition from Moses and all the prophets that day, as Jesus taught the things concerning himself!)

But something took place immediately as they recognized their risen Lord:

III. Their Experience Brought:

A. *A genuine faith* (v. 31). "And they knew him." They saw that this world's seeming triumphs are not final, not real—that Jesus can be depended upon.

B. *Real joy and hope* (v. 32). "Did not our hearts burn within us?" They saw that they had a share in Christ's triumph. They could not then know all the implications, but it began to dawn, then, of the scope of Jesus' victory over death.

C. *An irrepressible desire to share* (v. 33). "They rose up the same hour, and returned to Jerusalem." Seven miles on foot after dark—they just couldn't wait until morning!

Conclusion

Have you ever been like those two disciples on the Emmaus Road—sad, discouraged, perhaps even without faith and hope? It could be that someone has a faith that is in the *past* tense. "I trusted, but my heart has been broken; I have been failed!"

Where do you suppose Jesus is right *now*?

He is nearer than you think. And in just the same way that He revealed himself to Mary, and to the Eleven and to these two on the way, He will reveal himself to you. Will you respond to the thing that you know in your heart He would have you do?

Our Living Lord

TEXT: *Who is he that condemneth? It is Christ that died, yea rather, that is risen again, who is even at the right hand of God, who also maketh intercession for us* (Rom. 8:34).

In the climax of this great chapter on the triumph of the Spirit-filled life, Paul, in a single, simple sentence outlines all that we are celebrating this Easter morning! Christ *died;* Christ is *risen;* Christ is *ascended to glory;* and Christ makes *intercession for us!*

I. Christ Died

A. With every other man it would be a great wonder if he did not die; with Jesus it is truly remarkable that He *did* die. By His own words, "No one takes [my life] from me, but I lay it down of my own accord" (John 10:18, RSV). This death was *unique.*

B. Christ's death was a triumph of *love.* "Greater love hath no man than this, that a man lay down his life for his friends" (John 15:13).

C. Christ's death was a mighty, effective *redemption.* "By his own blood he entered in once into the holy place, having obtained eternal redemption for us" (Heb. 9:12). But Paul hurries to add:

II. Christ Is Risen

A. A personal triumph, a vindication of His *integrity.* As Peter said, in passing, in his great inaugural sermon, "It was impossible that death should hold him" (Acts 2:24, TEV).

B. But much, much more: a *triumph* for the whole

race (a whole new race). "But now is Christ risen from the dead, and become the firstfruits of them that slept" (1 Cor. 15:20).

C. And yet this triumph is not just for the future, for eternity, when we die. His resurrection ushered in a *new order;* it was not just a return to life and then "business as usual."

For Paul continues:

III. Christ Is Ascended to Glory

A. Christ came to do a task. He came to die, to defeat sin and hell; and having finished that task, He *assumed again the power* that was rightfully His. "I have finished the work which thou gavest me to do. And now, O Father, glorify thou me with thine own self with the glory which I had with thee before the world was" (John 17:4-5).

B. Returned to glory! This dazzling brilliance is hard for us to comprehend. The risen Lord is the *same, yet* somehow gloriously *different!*

1. He must be spiritually discerned/revealed; for example, Peter, Mary, Cleopas, the closed Upper Room.

2. He is *awesome,* even to the beloved (Rev. 1:8, 17).

But perhaps best of all:

IV. Christ Makes Intercession for Us

In the power at the center of the universe, this risen Christ is engaged in this great work.

A. Jesus is now *identified* with us. He became like us so that we may be like Him. "Beloved, now are we the sons of God . . . we know that, when he shall appear, we shall be like him" (1 John 3:2).

B. At the throne we are *loved.* Rom. 8:35 (the next verse after our text) asks: "Who shall separate us from the love of Christ?"

C. We are *prayed for* at the throne. Not just for power over death (which is in itself tremendous), but power over spiritual death and separation.

Conclusion

Because Christ lives, we have all the provision necessary to live the power of the Resurrection here and now!

These are the simple, profound facts of Easter: Jesus died, He is risen, He is seated in glory, and He makes intercession for us so that nothing can ever separate us from His love!

PRAYER: "Worthy is the Lamb! . . . Blessing, and honour, and glory, and power, be unto him that sitteth upon the throne and unto the Lamb for ever and ever. . . . Amen!" (See Rev. 5:12-14.)

EUGENE L. STOWE is one of six general superintendents of the Church of the Nazarene, a position he has filled since 1968. He was born in Council Bluffs, Ia., and graduated from Pasadena College in Pasadena, Calif. His ministerial career has included pastorates in Visalia and Oakland, Calif.; Salem, Ore.; and Nampa, Ida. During his pastorate at Nampa College Church he also taught for six years in the Department of Religion of Northwest Nazarene College. He served as district superintendent of the Central California District for two years. It was while he was president of Nazarene Theological Seminary that he was elected general superintendent. In recognition of his outstanding service to the church, Pasadena College conferred an honorary doctoral degree in 1966.

Dr. Stowe was general president of the Nazarene Young People's Society from 1956 to 1960, during which time he was a member of the General Board. He is the author of *The Spiritual Glow* and *The Ministry of Shepherding*.

PENTECOST

Eugene L. Stowe

Perhaps no day on the Christian calendar has been more misunderstood and maligned than Pentecost. E. Stanley Jones once stated that by and large the Church was lost somewhere between Easter and Pentecost. What a tragic commentary!

The event which took place in the Upper Room in Jerusalem 50 days after the Passover was as well documented historically as was the day of Christ's resurrection. This was as clearly the inauguration of the dispensation of the Holy Spirit as the advent of Jesus was the opening of the Christian era.

Those who deny this truth invariably have real problems with the doctrine of the Holy Spirit. This brings to mind a humorous children's story which has an all too serious application in the lives of many adult Christians. A children's catechism class was learning the Apostles' Creed. Each child had been assigned a sentence to repeat. The first one said, "I believe in God the Father Almighty, Maker of heaven and earth." The second stated, "I believe in Jesus Christ, His only Son . . ." When he had completed his sentence, there was an embarrassing silence. Finally, one child piped up, "Teacher, the boy who believes in the Holy Ghost is not here." And all too many Christians who do not comprehend the meaning of Pentecost are caught in this same dilemma.

In recent years those who call themselves Pentecostals have moved into this void and exploited the phenomenon of speaking in languages. This subscriptural emphasis upon ecstatic, emotional extremism has created a strong bias against the whole subject of Pentecost in the minds of many Christians. This negative image compelled the 1919 General Assembly of the Church of the Nazarene to remove the term *Pentecostal* from its official title.

But all this confusion and lack of understanding only makes it more imperative that proper attention be paid to this day on which the Christian Church was born. The problem areas should be faced frankly. However, the major thrust should be a positive, biblical approach to the major meaning of Pentecost.

There are two major premises which should be firmly established:

1. *The historic Christian Pentecost was a not-to-be-repeated event.* In Judaism, Pentecost was one of the three great feast days which was observed annually to celebrate the wheat harvest. But the Jerusalem Pentecost which took place after the Passover-fulfilling death of Jesus was totally different. The phenomenal signs which were observed in the Upper Room and on the streets of the city identified this as a very special occasion. The Third Person of the Trinity "went public" in the lives of the 120 disciples who were "filled with the Holy Spirit" (Acts 2:4, NASB). Like the Bethlehem star and the angelic choir which announced the birth of Christ, these sights and sounds were nonreproducible, just as was the occasion which they accompanied.

2. *A personal Pentecost is the birthright of every born-again believer.* The infilling of the Spirit is for us all today. One need not travel to the Holy Land to find this fullness. It can take place in Jacksonville or Joplin just as surely as it did in Jerusalem! Charles H. Gabriel's gospel

64

hymn entitled "Pentecostal Power" speaks of this present-day possibility:

> Lord, as of old at Pentecost
> Thou didst Thy pow'r display,
> With cleansing, purifying flame
> Descend on us today.
>
> For mighty works for Thee, prepare
> And strengthen ev'ry heart.
> Come, take possession of Thine own,
> And nevermore depart.

I have always believed in series preaching. Great scriptural themes cannot often be adequately dealt with in one message. And expository preaching (which Paul Rees contends is the only real preaching) lends itself naturally to a series of messages on a particular passage of Scripture.

Two of the meaningful traditions of my pastoral ministry were the annual sermon series at the Christmas and Lenten seasons. For 10 years in my last pastorate I preached four Sunday mornings, and sometimes Sunday evenings as well, on themes relating to these significant occasions. In looking back, I believe that these were high points in my pulpit ministry; for the preacher, I'm sure, and I trust for the people.

However, in retrospect I believe that I did not give sufficient sermonic attention to Pentecost. There was always an appropriate message on that Sunday morning in which I spoke to the major meaning of the day. But if I were doing it again, I would give "equal time" to Pentecost. Three or four sermons leading up to or following this day would have given my people a fuller understanding of the vital importance and spiritual significance of Pentecost both then and now.

The brief outlines which follow are presented with the prayer that some practicing pastors and evangelists may be challenged to undertake a program of series preaching at Pentecost. Under God it might well precipitate another outpouring of the Holy Spirit which can become a virtual "birth-day" in many churches, just as it did for that first Church on that first Christian Pentecost.

Pentecost—The Real Thing

SERIES SCRIPTURE: Acts 2:1-4

SERMON TEXT: *And when the day of Pentecost had come . . . they were all filled with the Holy Spirit* (2:1, 4, NASB).

Pentecost is the last of the three greatest days on the Christian calendar. The first, of course, is Christmas—the celebration of Christ's birth. The second is Easter—the celebration of Christ's resurrection. And the third is Pentecost—the celebration of the outpouring of the Holy Spirit.

I. But to Fully Understand What Happened on This Significant Day, We Must Have an Understanding of the Old Testament Meaning of Pentecost.

A. The literal meaning of the word is "50 days," and it was positioned on the Jewish calendar seven weeks after the Passover.

B. It was the Jewish feast of harvest and was equivalent to our Thanksgiving Day. The high point of the celebration was the bringing of two loaves of bread, made from the newly harvested wheat, which were presented to the priest. This symbolized the dedication of the harvest to God, and no produce was eaten until this ceremony was held.

C. The deeper meaning of the Old Testament Pentecost was symbolic. From our vantage point as Christians we can understand the beautiful parallel between the Jewish feast and its New Testament fulfillment.

1. *Christ's death at Calvary completed the typology of the Passover.* Just as the blood of the lamb delivered the Israelite from the death angel's terrible visitation, so the blood of Jesus, the Lamb of God, saves from spiritual death.

2. *The consecration of the bread signifies the personal commitment at Pentecost.* As the loaves were presented to the priest, so the disciples' lives were offered completely to God in the Upper Room. Listen to the words of Acts 1:14, "These all with one mind were continually devoting themselves to prayer" (NASB). They were already believers. In John 17, Jesus had testified that they were not of the world. They were certainly not praying to be converted. This 10-day prayer marathon must have witnessed the emptying of themselves so that they could receive the fullness of the Holy Spirit. And this same total commitment is an integral part of the sanctifying work of the Spirit in one's personal Pentecost. This is the sum and substance of Paul's exhortation to the Roman Christians: "Therefore, I urge you, brothers, in view of God's mercy, to offer your bodies as living sacrifices, holy and pleasing to God" (12:1, NIV). As we prepare for Pentecost, let the call to complete consecration come loud and clear to every modern-day disciple who comes to the Upper Room.

II. Then We Must Understand that the First Christian Pentecost Was the Fulfillment of Prophetic Promise.

A. Peter, the preacher on Pentecost Day, left no doubt in anyone's mind about this:

"This is what was spoken of through the prophet Joel:
'And it shall be in the last days,' God says,

'That I will pour forth of My Spirit upon all mankind;
And your sons and your daughters shall prophesy,
And your young men shall see visions,
And your old men shall dream dreams;
Even upon My bondslaves, both men and women,
I will in those days pour forth of My Spirit
And they shall prophesy. . . .
'And it shall be, that every one who calls on the name
   of the Lord shall be saved.' ' "

(Acts 2:16-18, 21, NASB)

Thank God, the Comforter has come! Now all three Persons of the Godhead—Father, Son, and Holy Spirit—have been fully revealed and released to the world. Let us receive this glorious truth with glad and obedient hearts and avail ourselves of the full resources of the outpoured Spirit.

III. Finally, the Baptism with the Holy Spirit at Pentecost Confirmed the Predictions of Jesus and John the Baptist.

A. In Mark 1:8 and Luke 3:16, John, the forerunner of Christ, testified that he baptized with water, but One mightier than he would baptize them with the Holy Spirit. Luke remembers him saying that this baptism would be "with the Holy Spirit and fire." Pentecost proved that he was right.

B. Then the Master ratified John's forecast in the bold prophecy recorded in Acts 1:4-5: "He commanded them . . . to wait for what the Father had promised, 'Which,' He said, 'you heard of from Me; for John baptized with water, but you shall be baptized with the Holy Spirit not many days from now' " (NASB). Jesus always keeps His promise, and Pentecost is one more strong proof of that fact.

Conclusion

Pentecost is a verifiable historical happening. But it is more than ancient history. The Father still promises to give the Holy Spirit to them that ask Him (Luke 11:13). The Pentecostal baptism is still ours for the asking. It is the sanctifying fullness to which every born-again believer is entitled and which is desperately needed to add the final dimension to his or her discipleship.

One does not need to wait until Pentecost Sunday to receive the baptism with the Holy Spirit. Pray this prayer with the songwriter and be filled just now:

> Hover o'er me, Holy Spirit,
>   Bathe my trembling heart and brow;
> Fill me with Thy hallowed presence,
>   Come, O come and fill me now.
>
> Thou canst fill me, gracious Spirit,
>   Though I cannot tell Thee how;
> But I need Thee, greatly need Thee;
>   Come, O come and fill me now.

("Fill Me Now" by Elwood H. Stokes)

Pentecost Means Purity

Series Scripture: Acts 2:1-4, NASB: *And when the day of Pentecost had come, they were all together in one place. And suddenly there came from heaven a noise like a violent, rushing wind, and it filled the whole house where they were sitting. And there appeared to them tongues as of fire distributing themselves, and they rested on each one of them. And they were all filled with the Holy Spirit and began to speak with other tongues, as the Spirit was giving them utterance.*

SERMON TEXT: Matt. 3:11-12, NASB: *I baptize you in water for repentance, but He who is coming after me is mightier than I. . . . He Himself will baptize you with the Holy Spirit and fire. And His winnowing fork is in His hand, and He will thoroughly clean His threshing floor; and He will gather His wheat into the barn, but He will burn up the chaff with unquenchable fire.*

Introduction

When God's Word says it once, that makes that truth important. But when it states it twice in almost exactly the same language, that makes it doubly important. In today's scripture we find Matthew reporting the very same words that Luke heard John the Baptist say (Luke 3:16-17). This indicates that the Holy Spirit felt this truth was so vital that He inspired two of the synoptic writers to record it. In both instances John predicts not only the baptism with the Holy Spirit but specifies that this will be a baptism with fire. The reason is readily apparent.

I. Water Baptism Was Then and Is Now Associated with Forgiveness.

John said, "I indeed baptize you with water unto repentance" (Matt. 3:11a). His disciples had confessed and forsaken their sins and were witnessing to their conversion by submitting to baptism. At Pentecost Peter exhorted his non-Christian hearers to "repent, and be baptized every one of you in the name of Jesus Christ for the remission of sins" (Acts 2:38).

Modern believers should also demonstrate publicly their renunciation of sin and "acceptance of the benefits of the atonement of Jesus Christ" (*Manual*, Church of the Nazarene, Article XIII, Articles of Faith). This sacrament testifies to a complete break with the old sinful life-style. While it is meaningful in predominantly Christian cultures, it has even greater significance in world areas where the major religions are pagan. New Christians who undergo baptism in a lake or river declare their faith in no uncertain terms.

But John boldly declares that Christ will bring a second baptism. It is completely unique to Christianity. Dr. Ralph Earle states, "Other religions have baptized with water. The distinctive Christian baptism is that with the Holy Spirit" (*Beacon Bible Commentary*, 6:50).

II. This Fiery Baptism Accomplishes the Complete Cleansing and Purifying of the Christian.

A. Throughout the Old Testament, fire is repeatedly identified as the agent of cleaning. Isaiah's lips were cleansed and his sin purged by a coal of fire from the altar (6:6-7). Mal. 3:2-3 speaks of this purification in these words: "For he is like a refiner's fire . . . and he shall sit as a refiner and purifier of silver: and he shall purify the sons of Levi." Zech. 13:9 reads, "And I will bring the third part through the fire, and will refine them as silver is refined."

B. It is more than coincidence that the second symbolic phenomenon at Pentecost was the tongues of fire which rested on the heads of the 120. The message was clear. The fire of the Holy Spirit's baptism would purify their hearts and purge their natures of the inbred sin which is not forgivable but is cleansable. And He did!

C. Peter is living proof that Pentecost means purity. His carnal, cowardly heart which had motivated his denial of his Master was touched by the cleansing fire of the Holy Spirit. Self-will was crucified. Self-aggrandizement was burned out. The old man was replaced by a brand-new man. Never again, even under the threat of death, would he deny

71

his Lord. Listen to his testimony at the Jerusalem "General Assembly"—"God . . . showed that he accepted them [the Gentiles] by giving the Holy Spirit to them, just as he did to us. He made no distinction between us and them, for he purified their hearts by faith" (Acts 15:8-9, NIV). Heart cleansing made the difference. Pentecost—both the Jewish and Gentile—meant purity.

D. This is no sectarian dogma. It is the clear teaching of Scripture. No less. a biblical scholar than the great G. Campbell Morgan gives the weight of his authority to this truth when he paraphrases the Baptist's words in this way: "He shall whelm you in the fire-whelming of the Holy Ghost, that *burns your sin out of you*" (*The Gospel According to Matthew* [New York: Fleming H. Revell Co., 1929], p. 23). One of the beautiful Wesley hymns prays for this Pentecostal purity:

> *Come, Holy Ghost, all quickening fire!*
> *My consecrated heart inspire,*
> *When wilt Thou my whole heart subdue?*
> *Come, Lord, and form my soul anew,*
> *Emptied of pride, and wrath, and hell.*

This is the birthright of every believer.

III. And the Bible Makes It Plain that It Is Cleansing Fire Now or Unquenchable Fire Later.

Old-timers used to preach a great deal on "Holiness or Hell." That may seem highly unsophisticated in this day, but they were spelling out the alternatives. Biblical scholars are agreed that Matt. 3:12 has a dual meaning. Initially the cleansing of the threshing floor and the burning of the chaff refers to the purifying of the believer's heart by the fiery baptism with the Holy Spirit.

But just as surely, this passage points to the final consummation when sinful chaff will be destroyed with "unquenchable fire." This sobering truth is borne out by Heb. 12:14: "Follow peace with all men, and holiness, without which no man shall see the Lord." In this light the cleansing of entire sanctification is not optional but absolutely imperative.

Just as the early disciples obediently submitted themselves to the purging of Pentecost, even so must Christians today tarry for the crucifixion of the carnal nature and the consequent blessing of a pure heart. Let us pray with the songwriter:

> *Oh make me clean, Oh make me clean,*
> *Mine eyes Thy holiness have seen.*
> *Now send the burning, cleansing flame,*
> *And make me clean, In Jesus' name.*

("Oh Make Me Clean" by George Bennard)

Pentecost Means Power

SERIES SCRIPTURE: Acts 2:1-4, NIV: *When the day of Pentecost came, they were all together in one place. Suddenly a sound like the blowing of a violent wind came from heaven and filled the whole house where they were sitting. They saw what seemed to be tongues of fire that separated and came to rest on each of them. All of them were filled with the Holy Spirit and began to speak in other tongues [or languages] as the Spirit enabled them.*

SERMON TEXT: Acts 1:8, NIV: *But you will receive power when the Holy Spirit comes on you; and you will be my witnesses in Jerusalem, and in all Judea and Samaria, and to the ends of the earth.*

Introduction

Dr. Phineas F. Bresee frequently stated that the church can be likened to a rowboat which is propelled by two oars. One oar is Pentecostal purity and the other is Pentecostal power. Anyone who has ever rowed a boat knows that if only one oar is used, the boat will revolve aimlessly in circles. Of if one oar is pulled more strongly than the other, the boat will veer off its course and will head in another direction. Said Dr. Bresee, if the church is to keep on its biblically directed course, we must exert the same pull on both oars. Equal emphasis must be placed upon both purity and power.

Traditionally Calvinists have stressed power almost to the neglect of purity. But just as traditionally, Wesleyan-Arminians have majored in the preaching of heart purity and too often minored in the aspect of power. Perhaps that is one reason why so many churches have drifted off course and some even have ended up going in circles.

I. Just as Surely as Pentecost Produced Purity, It Was Also a Baptism of Power

A. Jesus clearly promised this in Acts 1:8. His disciples were suffering from a real power shortage. In fact, it was an energy crisis! His resurrection had restored His credibility with them, but now they were staggered by the immensity of the assignment which He had given them—"go and make disciples of all nations" (Matt. 28:19a, NIV). It was all they could do to survive. Verse 17 reports that "when [the Eleven] saw him, they worshiped him; but some doubted" (NIV). How can doubtful disciples be dynamic enough to make any other disciples, to say nothing of evangelizing "all nations"?

B. What a difference Pentecost made! The phenomenal sound "like the blowing of a violent wind" (Acts 2:2a) was the sign of the mighty power of the Spirit. No tornado or hurricane could equal the omnipotence which was being released.

1. This promised baptism of power was the final dimension of their transformation. In fact, they literally became "transformers." In the field of electricity the transformer is the instrument which transforms high-voltage electrical current into a level of voltage which can perform useful service. Pentecostal purity had opened up the conduits of their lives until they could become "transformers" of the high-voltage power of the Spirit. Instead of short-circuiting God's power, now they became conductors of it.

2. A prime example was the deacon named Philip. He probably would have identified himself as "just a layman," as so many of our good laymen still do. But in Acts 8 we find the thrilling story of how in the Spirit's power he went down to a Samaritan city and precipitated a real city-wide revival. As he lifted up Christ, scores of men and women became believers and were baptized. But in addition, cripples were healed, demons were exorcised, and "there was great joy in that city" (v. 8).

II. The Evidence Is Very Clear that the Power Released at Pentecost Was Primarily for Witnessing

A. Certainly the fullness of the Spirit energized the disciples for victorious Christian living. And on occasion miracles and other spiritual phenomena accompanied their post-Pentecost ministry. But in Acts 1:8 Christ specified that the power which they would receive when the Holy Spirit came upon them would equip them to "be *my* witnesses."

1. The power to speak in other languages was the power to witness. It was not an ecstatic, emotional "high." They were enabled in the power of the Spirit to tell who

Jesus was and what He had done in their lives through the medium of languages which were completely foreign to them. People from 16 other countries immediately heard the Good News and became candidates for conversion.

There is strong evidence that this was the third and last of the phenomenal signs accompanying the dispensational outpouring of the Holy Spirit. It symbolized the worldwide scope of the gospel which could not be confined to Jerusalem, Judea, or even Samaria, but must be published to the "ends of the earth" (Acts 1:8d, NIV). Thousands of missionary trainees wish that God would do it again! But trainees from "Pentecostal" churches which believe in tongues-speaking study in language schools alongside those from noncharismatic communions.

2. Through the Spirit's power the bashful became bold. So powerful was the witness of Preacher Peter and the other 119 that before the Day of Pentecost was over, about 3,000 were converted. But it did not stop there. In Acts 7 we hear the strong witness of Stephen who was "full . . . of the Holy Spirit" (6:5a, NIV). It pierced the heart of a young Pharisee named Saul, who was there giving approval to Stephen's death, and doubtless contributed to his conversion.

III. This Same Spiritual Power for Witnessing Is Still Available

A. Every Christian will not be an evangelist. According to Eph. 4:11 this is a spiritual gift which is bestowed by the sovereign wisdom and will of God on those whom He chooses. *But every Christian should be a witness.* None in the Upper Room were exempted. They were *all* filled, and they *all* became His witnesses.

B. Today, those who in complete consecration open their lives to the Spirit's baptism will receive this witnessing power. But it is given to be used. Halford Luccock rightly observes that "the disciples received the Pentecostal power when they faced the Pentecostal task." And we will too.

Mary Q did. Widowed at the age of 75, she reached out to Christ and found salvation and the fullness of the Spirit. In three years her contagious witness brought 23 individuals to Christ.

> O Lord, send the power just now,
> And baptize every one.
> Amen.

Pentecost—The Week After

SERIES SCRIPTURE: Acts 2:1-4, NEB: *While the day of Pentecost was running its course they were all together in one place, when suddenly there came from the sky a noise like that of a strong driving wind, which filled the whole house where they were sitting. And there appeared to them tongues like flames of fire, dispersed among them and resting on each one. And they were all filled with the Holy Spirit and began to talk in other tongues, as the Spirit gave them power of utterance.*

SERMON TEXT: Acts 2:42, 46-47; 4:31, NEB: *They met constantly to hear the apostles teach, and to share the common life, to break bread, and to pray. . . . With one mind they kept up their daily attendance at the temple, and, breaking bread in private houses, shared their meals with unaffected joy, as they praised God and enjoyed the favour of the whole people. And day by day the Lord added to their number those whom he was saving. . . . When they had ended their prayer, . . . all were filled with the Holy Spirit and spoke the word of God with boldness.*

Introduction

The Day of Pentecost had come and gone. Now what? Was it just to be "business as usual"? The passages of Scripture which we have just read strongly indicate that Pentecost had both perpetuated and precipitated some very important changes in the life-style of those who had been filled with the Holy Spirit. Let us give our attention to several very apparent differences which were demonstrated in the week after.

I. Now They Did Not Just Attend the Church—They Were the Church. Now They Were Not Just a Band of Believers—They Were the Body of Christ.

The Church had been born in the Upper Room. And what dynamic Body life it immediately began to demonstrate.

A. *The means of grace were a daily delight.*

1. They didn't just go to the synagogue on the Sabbath; "they kept up their *daily* attendance at the temple" (2:46, NEB, italics added). There is something suspect about any supposedly Christian movement which directs its people away from the institutional church.

2. But this was not enough. The King James Version translates verse 42, "And they continued steadfastly in the apostles' doctrine . . . and in prayers." The *New English Bible* makes it even clearer: "They met constantly to hear the apostles teach . . . and to pray." No one had to beg or threaten to get them to prayer meeting! The prayer vigil in the Upper Room had produced life-changing results, and now it had become their way of life. And just as babies crave food constantly, so these new Christians had an insatiable appetite for spiritual truth.

3. Pentecost produced this same difference more than a millennium later. Church history records that on August 13, 1727, some 300 Moravian Brethren at Communion in Berthelsdorf witnessed another Pentecost. One who was there reported that "everyone there desired more than anything else that the Holy Spirit might have control. Self-love and self-will, as well as all disobedience, disappeared. There was such a hunger for the Word of God that we had to have services daily at 5 and 7:30 a.m. and 9 p.m."

B. *The second cardinal characteristic was the unbroken fellowship which they enjoyed.*

1. The adhesive which bound them together was what Paul identifies as the "unity of the Spirit" (Eph. 4:3). These people seemed to be hopelessly divided by their cultural, economic, and intellectual differences, but they were gloriously united as members of the Body of Christ. They wanted to be together as much as possible "to share the common life" (2:42*b*, NEB). They ate together. They praised God together. They were even willing to pool their possessions in a common treasury (2:44). If they had known the gospel hymn "Onward, Christian Soldiers," their favorite stanza would no doubt have been the one which contains these words:

We are not divided;
All one body we.

2. Small wonder that this fellowship produced "unaffected joy" (2:46*c*, NEB). Such Pentecostal togetherness will still provide such a spirit in today's church. Christianity was never intended to be a long-faced litany. One of the choicest fruits of the Spirit is holy joy.

C. *Last but certainly not least, they demonstrated conclusively that church growth is the natural consequence of real Body life.*

1. *Their fellowship became contagious.* They "enjoyed the favour of the whole people" (2:47b, NEB). Koinonia is attractive. People still hunger for real New Testament fellowship. And the word will get around when a church has it.

2. *Their witness for Christ was constant.* One Bible scholar insists that the real meaning of Acts 8:4 is best rendered, "they . . . went everywhere *gossiping* the gospel." Peter and John obviously stated the truth when they declared, "We cannot but speak the things which we have seen and heard" (Acts 4:20). Jesus was so real and the Spirit was so powerful that it just came naturally for them to "gossip" the gospel.

3. Small wonder that "day by day the Lord added to their number those whom he was saving" (2:47c, NEB). This was the first "Evangelism Explosion." It need not be the last. These same causes will still produce the same effects. When the modern Church experiences a genuine Pentecost, the weeks after will still witness dynamic church growth.

II. The Week After Pentecost Also Established the Fact that There Are Subsequent Fresh Fillings of the Spirit for Those Who Have Received the Initial Baptism.

A. The evidence is very clear in Acts 4:31—they "all were filled with the Holy Spirit" (NEB). Many if not almost all of these disciples had received the sanctifying fullness at Pentecost. Subsequent events conclusively proved that they had not lost the blessing or the Blesser.

B. Faced with nearly impossible demands and clearly articulated opposition, they sensed the need for a new infilling of that same Spirit. Not a charismatic supercharge nor a third work of grace, but a fresh touch, a new anointing.

80

And it came! And it so energized them that they "spoke the word of God with boldness" (4:31*b*, NEB).

C. And one of the surest signs that we have experienced a genuine Pentecost is that we very naturally hunger for such subsequent fresh fillings of the Spirit. The Church faces unparalleled demands in the 80s. A personal Pentecost is still the only adequate initial power source for the Christian. But we may have all of the Holy Spirit that our needs demand. With this strong enablement the Church will again be the Church that Christ intended.

LESLIE PARROTT is president of Olivet Nazarene College in Kankakee, Ill., a position he has held since 1975. Prior to his present assignment he was president of Eastern Nazarene College for five years. He served as pastor in Kelso, Wash.; Flint, Mich.; Kirkland, Wash.; and Portland, Ore. He holds the A.B. degree from Olivet Nazarene College; the M.A. from Willamette University; and the Ph.D. from Michigan State University.

Dr. Parrott has travelled widely and is a featured speaker at conferences and camp meetings across the land. In addition, his prolific writings and many books have ministered effectively to a large audience. Some of his books are: *The Art of Happy Christian Living, The Power of Your Attitudes, What Is Sanctification? Building Today's Church, Perspectives in Bible Holiness,* and *Sons of Africa.*

BACCALAUREATE

Leslie Parrott

The sermon expectations of the congregation change from ordinary Sundays to something else when people gather for the baccalaureate service. I doubt if the people and especially the students know what they expect, but they do know the service will be different.

For instance, (1) the graduates will be dressed in caps and gowns, seated down front, consecutively, in rows. (2) The parents may focus their attention more on students than the sermon. (3) Everyone is more self-conscious than usual. (4) The service will be more ceremonial than usual. (5) And, often, the principal or superintendent of schools who is in charge is not likely to be a minister and may be uncomfortable in his or her role in the service.

The minister needs to decide several things before preparation of the sermon begins. (1) Will the message be an address, a sermon, or a sermon prepared in the form of an address? The usual Bible sermon which depends on a close following of the congregation with their own Bibles is not always practical in a baccalaureate service since many people will not have Bibles with them. (2) How long will the message be? More baccalaureate sermons are too long than too short. (3) Will the preacher be in academic garb, and if so, how can he prepare himself in advance to be comfortable and free in his speaking?

(4) Will notes be used, or will the sermon be read from a manuscript, or delivered extemporaneously? Most of us do

not read well in public; and if the people are accustomed to an extemporaneous message, they may feel uncomfortable listening to a manuscript. I have tried the straight scriptural message and found I was the only one on the platform or among the students who brought his Bible. I finally evolved my approach to an extemporaneous delivery of a baccalaureate sermon each year which dealt with some theme I thought would capture the imagination of the students and give me a chance to deliver biblical truth in a way which would stick in their minds.

In the last 10 years of preaching baccalaureate sermons in Nazarene colleges I have closely coordinated the music and the message. But in high schools and community colleges where I have had less control over the service, the following sermon starters have been typical of the kinds of messages I have tried to give.

One final word about titles. Many public high schools and junior colleges are reluctant to promote or require attendance at baccalaureate services. But several times they have asked me in advance for the title of my message. One junior college president told me he was sure that the announcement of my sermon title, "The Beat Generation and the Angry Young Men," had been a significant factor in the larger-than-usual attendance at a Sunday afternoon baccalaureate service in a fine arts auditorium. The more your title relates to concerns and interests among students, the higher will be the level of anticipation and expectation for your sermon.

The Teacher and the Transformed Life

In the small Massachusetts town of Southbridge there was an angry boy who made trouble for everyone whose life he touched. The only exceptions were the other angry boys in the gang with whom he found his identity.

Bill Marcy was resentful toward all adults, especially authority figures, and specifically schoolteachers. His little bunch of hoodlums were a personal mafia which he led into all kinds of mischief. All the concerned mothers told their sons to stay away from Bill Marcy because he was no good. With a mixture of threat and compassion, they said, "He will only grow up to fill a hangman's noose or rot away in a prison someplace."

This angry boy listened to this kind of talk until he believed it himself and started out to live up to his reputation. One spring day his little gang of hoodlums broke up the village school and ran the schoolmaster out of town.

In the summer the school board hired a new teacher. When he arrived in September, the whole town sat back to see who would win, Bill Marcy and his gang or the new schoolteacher, Salem Towne.

Not long after school began, the whole town was shocked one day to see this big, overgrown boy, Bill Marcy, walking down the street, arm in arm, with the new schoolteacher. The two became fast friends. Bill's entire set of attitudes and personal behavior patterns were changed and his life transformed.

That boy in whom no one saw any good grew up to be a United States senator. For three terms in succession he was governor of the state of New York. And finally he became the secretary of state of the United States.

When he died, there were 100,000 people who filed by

to see his body as it lay in state. And the state of New York, wanting to do something to honor the memory of Bill Marcy, named the tallest mountain in New York State, Mount Marcy.

One day when the governor of Massachusetts was having a reception for the Hon. Wm. Marcy, it so happened that Salem Towne, the former schoolteacher who had now risen to become state superintendent of public instruction, was present. When the governor started to introduce the two men, he saw immediately that they knew one another. When the governor asked the men how they knew each other, the Hon. Wm. Marcy replied, "This man literally transformed my life. When I was an angry, resentful boy trying to spite the world by destroying my life, he got through to me. All I am or have ever done I owe to him."

To understand what happened to Bill Marcy, it is necessary to understand that three interacting factors make each of us what we are. First, there is the *biological factor*. The fact that you are a man or woman is no insignificant difference. The biological factor has to do with physical appearance, strength, stamina, and tendency toward certain diseases. For the most part it determines intelligence. The biological factor does not guarantee personal development to the limit of our strength or intelligence, but it does set the ceiling.

The second factor which makes us what we are is *environment*. The fact of a birth into an Anglo-Saxon, Caucasian, middle-class American home makes one child eternally different from a child born in an Eastern European family, living in the Jewish ghetto of Warsaw. By the time a child can speak the language of the culture into which he is born, he is the victim of it.

But the third factor which makes each of us what we are is the *inner self*. This soul of man is to be reckoned with. It can overcome the biological and environmental factors or be victimized by them. The inner self has great adaptability and elasticity, or it can be brittle and unbending. It can be strong or weak, angry or loving, rigid or adjustable. And it is in this inner self that an amazing transformation can be performed. In fact, when the inner self is transformed, it even makes a difference in the biological and environmental factors.

In the case of Bill Marcy, the *biological factor* was changed little, if any. The *environment* was left the same. The schoolhouse was on the same plot of ground; and the same adult faces were reflected in the storefronts on Main Street. The real transformation was in the *inner self*. Through the transformation of the inner man, Bill Marcy actually became a different person. Salem Towne was used of God in guiding Bill Marcy through the process which developed within him (1) a new identity, (2) a new self-respect, and finally (3) a new set of ideals and aspirations.

The writer of Hebrews said that God has made a new covenant with man: "For this is the covenant that I will make with the house of Israel after those days, said the Lord; I will put my laws into their mind, and write them in their hearts; and I will be to them a God, and they shall be to me a people" (8:10). This is the covenant of the transformed soul, the inner self. God does not transform your life by making you taller or shorter, or 20 pounds heavier or lighter. He does not transform your life by lifting you out of an unfavorable environment and setting you down in a better one. He transforms your life by transforming (1) your mind, (2) your will, and (3) your emotions, your inner self.

I. Jesus Christ Can Work Through Your Life to Give You a New Identity.

Throughout the Bible there are examples of God giving men new names during some great spiritual event. When

God renewed His covenant with *Abram*, He changed his name to *Abraham*. At the same time God promised his wife *Sarai*—90 years of age and without a child—a son; and God changed her name to *Sarah* (Genesis 17). When Jacob the deceiver wrestled all night with the angel and faced up to his responsibility with his brother, God changed his name from *Jacob* to *Israel* (Genesis 32). When *Simon the fisherman* made the great confession—"Thou art the Christ, the Son of the living God"—Jesus changed his name to *Peter the rock* (Matt. 16:13-20). This changing of our personal identity must be what Jesus had in mind when He told Nicodemus, "Ye must be born again" (John 3).

II. Jesus Christ Can Transform Your Life by Giving You a New Self-respect.

The difference between Judas and Peter at one point was fairly small. Judas betrayed Jesus and Peter denied Him. Judas kissed Him hypocritically, and Peter cursed and blasphemed to prove he never had known Jesus. Judas even started back on the road to reconciliation by trying to make restitution. He tried to give back the money to the chief priests, but they wouldn't accept it. Overwhelmed in his complete loss of self-respect, Judas went out to commit suicide.

When Jesus came out of the tomb on Easter, His first instruction to the angel was to relay the command, "Go . . . tell his disciples *and Peter*" (Mark 16:7). He knew Peter's self-respect was at an all-time low. And Jesus was making special arrangements to be with him. Even the message sent by Christ through the angel and the women at the tomb had within it the therapy of forgiveness, which is the first step back on the road to a new self-respect.

III. Jesus Christ Can Transform Your Life Through a New Set of Ideals and Aspirations.

Saul of Tarsus was a rigid product of the letter of the Old Testament law. But Christ transformed his life and made him the Apostle to the Gentiles, preaching the spirit of the law but condemning the letter. Peter was a narrow-minded Jew who thought the gospel of Christ was for the chosen people. But in a vision on the housetop in Joppa, he became the means for the conversion of the Gentile Italian family in Cornelius' home.

Faith and Learning in a Secular World

My mental picture of education consists of two mighty rivers, each turbulent and strong, flowing unrelentingly through many generations of history until they finally converge into the powerful course of history called Western civilization.

These two mighty rivers which came together to form our culture are the secular culture of Greece and Rome on the one hand and the Hebrew/Christian religious heritage on the other. Our mission is to comprehend truth in the secular traditions of the Greek and Roman liberal arts while teaching full appreciation for truth in our Hebrew/Christian heritage.

The tendency in many classrooms is to appreciate one or the other of these rivers of knowledge, but not both. If the church always comes off second best in every classroom discussion, there is something wrong with someone's educational vision. But neither is the error corrected with a set of educational eyeglasses that cannot see truth in the physical and social sciences.

In more recent times another dimension has been added to secular education. This is education without values. From this educational perspective there are no absolutes outside the science laboratory. Even God is doubted and His revealed Word is not taken as the final authority. As Christians face the challenge of secular education in junior high, high school, college, and in life experiences, there are at least three ideas which need to be kept in good focus.

First, the answer to secular education is not to deny the importance of the arts and sciences to our lives. Rejecting the secular side of life would only result in a new dark age of the closed mind. Christians need to accept all truth as God's truth.

Second, the answer to education without values is not a denial of the liberal arts, but neither is it a takeover of the classroom and laboratory by those who would Christianize the curriculum. A history of Christianity is in order, but not a Christian history, nor a Christian sociology, nor a Christian mathematics. When an attempt is made to Christianize the curriculum, logic must be adjusted to fit theology, and history's timetable and the dimensions of the universe must be remeasured to conform with someone's interpretation of Genesis. Zealous Christians have always been tempted at two extremes in education: either to manipulate their data into Christian shape, or to ignore liberal arts for the contemplative life of the separatist community where the facts of faith are studied without the uncomfortable intrusions of the facts of life. To read Christ into the writings of Plato or to wrench Platonism out of the parables is unfair to Christ and to Plato.

Third, Christian students need to accept the contributions of our Graeco-Roman heritage in the liberal arts while we give full attention to the towering strength of our Judeo-Christian heritage. Christ crucified and risen was proclaimed without apology by Paul to the philosophers of Athens and to the practical politicians from Caesar's household in Rome.

John Wesley hammered out his theology on the three anvils of Scripture, reason, and the facts of human experience. He was asked one day what he would do if he found a fact of faith in the Bible that met the demands of reason but did not pass the test of human experience. He replied that he would go back to the Bible and start reading again. Faith is not really faith until it has been hammered out on the anvil of human experience.

In the year 203 A.D., when Demetrius was the bishop of Alexandria, he placed a young man by the name of Origen in charge of education in the diocese. Doubtless the bishop had no intention of starting an intellectual revolution, since that is not the sort of thing that bishops ordinarily do. But the man and the moment in history had arrived. The time was at hand when the church, still preaching the Word of God in all the power of its divine simplicity, had to move onward and outward into the complex world of human affairs where the claims of the gospel would have to be explained to the satisfaction of the Greek philosophers and Roman scholars.

In his own words, Origen tells of this exciting intellectual experience. "When I devoted myself to the Word, and the report of my proficiency went abroad, there came to me adherents of the various schools of thought, and men conversant with Greek learning, particularly with philosophy. It seemed therefore necessary that I should examine the doctrines of the schools and see what the philosophers had said concerning the truth." In these words Origen describes the beginning of the full-scale historic encounter between Christianity and the ancient world of intellects which was begun by Paul with the philosophers on Mars' Hill and by John at Ephesus. God's truth is truth wherever it is found. Antagonism, separatism, or even a closed mind is not faith's answer to learning. It is not the fear of truth but knowing truth which sets men free.

Dealing with the Generation Gap

One of the most easily observed facts on the world scene today is the generation gap. Three hundred years ago, the recalcitrant young men of Europe sailed away on ships far from the observing eyes of watchful parents, sometimes even to America, the New World. One hundred years ago, young men with an overdose of hostility carried six-shooters and acted out their aggression in barroom brawls and in shoot-outs with each other and with United States marshals.

Today the young people with the most radical reactions to adult authority have joined communes, protest marches, and various armies of liberation from Boston to Berkeley and from Frankfurt to Tokyo. With the support of each other, they flaunt every Christian value in middle-class society and write about it in their underground newspapers. Nonselective love, complete rejection of social responsibility, psychedelic art, military pacifism, and drug experimentation take the places of old-fashioned values like honesty, hard work, and patriotism.

As Iney Showertz said in *Harper's* magazine, a generation transition may be made in only two or three years. A first-year public school teacher was shaken by a third grader who asked, "How were things back in your time?" Every 15-year-old is painfully aware of how little his parents know about life. A ninth grader has infinitely more maturity than an eighth grader. And a college senior may refuse to ride in the same car with a sophomore unless it is on a date. A mother in her early 30s spoke in all sincerity when she told her pastor who had just barely gotten into his 40s, "You can't really understand the people of my generation." In a country which will soon have half its population 21 years of age or under, a man has entered the never-never land when he crosses the line of 30.

This generation gap causes no small number of problems. Viewpoints differ, standards of excellence continue to rise, traditional ways and means for achieving goals are questioned thoughtfully, and even the goals themselves. External authority is almost always suspect, and anything which is not communicated in the idiom of the day is ancient and therefore not necessarily binding on youthful minds which have been satiated on "new" math, television, celestial navigation, and the philosophy of situation ethics.

But in spite of all the problems created by the generation gap, it still is appropriate to consider seriously the admonition of Proverbs: "Remove not the ancient landmark, which thy fathers have set" (22:28). Speaking to the 1915 General Assembly, Dr. Bresee said, "Pertaining to things not essential to salvation, we have liberty. To attempt to emphasize that which is not essential to salvation and then divide forces, would be a crime." On nonessentials the generation gap makes an unmistakable difference. But in matters essential to eternal salvation there is and must be monolithic unity in the church. There are at least four ancient landmarks essential to salvation and held as viable in the church.

I. The First Ancient Landmark Is the Authority, Inspiration, and Inerrancy of the Scriptures in All Matters Pertaining to Salvation.

The Bible was not written as an authority on psychology, history, or economics. The purpose of the Bible

93

is to furnish all the information necessary to understand, to accept, to live, and to preach God's entire plan for redeeming men. In a word, the Bible is the authority on redemption to every person who is willing to be redeemed. The Bible is fully inspired and without error.

II. The Second Great Landmark of the Church Essential to Salvation Is "The Agreed Statement of Belief" in the "Manual."

This brief statement of only 188 words could be typewritten double spaced on less than one sheet of letter-writing paper. And yet it contains all matters of "belief as are essential to Christian experience." In plain, easily understood English, the church has stated profoundly the beliefs in one God, the inspiration of the Bible, the fallen nature of man, the atonement for the lost, sanctification, the witness of the Holy Spirit, and the second coming of Christ. No more and no less is needed.

III. The Third Old Landmark for All Generations Is the General Rules in the Constitution of the Church.

The men who hammered out these rules met in 1908 under a brown tent in Pilot Point, Tex. They drove horses and buggies and studied by the light of kerosene lamps. But don't sell them short. And don't rule them out as irrelevant because of your generation gap. In their own way, these rules are profound also. Who wants to quarrel with the rule which is to avoid evil of every kind such as profanity, desecration of Sunday, drinking liquor, quarreling, dishonesty, pride of dress, and songs, literature, and entertainments not to the glory of God? Or, who wants to quarrel with the rule which is to do that which is enjoined in the Word of God, including courtesy, contributing to the church, being helpful, loving God, attending church, seeking to do good to the needy, and pressing the claims of salvation on the lost? The third rule is no less profound in urging enthusiastic fellowship with the church. Maybe the three General Rules need more attention from people on both sides of the generation gap.

IV. And Finally, the Fourth Great Landmark of the Church of the Nazarene Is the Doctrine of Holiness.

If God can forgive, but not cleanse, His power over sin is limited. But from pulpits, in periodicals, personally, and persistently, the Church of the Nazarene proclaims salvation which is entire because the Bible teaches and men may experience fully the Holy Spirit, who is the mind of Christ in you.

The Shook-up Generation

One of the great perennial problems is what to do with the younger generation. And generations of adolescents coming along in the wake of great wars and other social upheavals seem to become intensified problems for their elders.

A. The generation of young people who went to high school and college during the Roaring 20s (which were produced by the social upheavals of World War I) were described by Ernest Hemingway, Gertrude Stein, and F. Scott Fitzgerald as "the lost generation."

B. Following World War II there was a new breed of teens and young adults which was referred to in England as "the angry young men" and in this country as "the beat generation." A newspaper reporter in San Francisco where these young people tended to gather in the North Bay Area called them "beatniks," and the title stuck. The beatnik rejected every middle-class Christian value and every authority figure in the community, including the preacher, the teacher, and the policeman. The beatnik carried existential philosophy to its ludicrous conclusion by stating his outlook on life in one sentence. In his anger, frustration, and futility he has declared, "Get out of my road and leave me alone to live and behave exactly as I want without any interference from present-day authority or any past standards of goodness." The beatnik has said, "I am not only the captain of my soul but the jury and the supreme court."

C. However, the beatnik wave is a thing of the past. Their own system of values has become so widely accepted we now have the "mod generation" with their far-out fashions and style of life. The spirit of revolt among today's younger generation is so well accepted, we use their rebellion as an advertising gimmick to sell Dodge automobiles. Now you can even get "rebellion" perfume.

D. But one of the best descriptions of today's young people is given by a Pulitzer Prize-winning journalist, Harrison Salisbury, of the *New York Times*. He calls this "The Shook-up Generation." And he says they are shook up because they live in a shook-up world. Their parents are shook-up products of World War II and are raising children in shook-up homes.

But really, the problem of what to do with the younger generation is not new. Listen to this: "The children now love luxury; they have bad manners, contempt for authority; they show disrespect for their elders and love chatter in place of exercise. They no longer rise when elders enter the room. They contradict their parents, chatter before company, gobble up the dainties at the table, cross their legs, and tyrannize their teachers." This was not written of today's shook-up generation. It was said by Socrates, 500 years before Christ.

But a wise old king who lived even before the days of Socrates saw the shook-up generation of his day and decided that all of life is vexation and vanity. He saw his generation was fighting the wind. The achievements of the elders were only a repeat of all that had been done, and there was no new thing under the sun. But having passed his judgment on the work of the adults in his generation, he gave some sage advice to the young adults. This advice, which might be called "the three Rs for youth," is in three successive verses of Ecclesiastes:

1. *"Rejoice,* O young man, in thy youth" (11:9).

2. *"Remove* sorrow from thy heart, and put away evil . . . for childhood and youth are vanity" (11:10).

3. *"Remember* now thy Creator in the days of thy youth, while the evil days come not" (12:1).

Reduced to its simplest form, this advice comes in three familiar words: (1) rejoice, (2) remove, and (3) remember.

The first directive to young people from this ancient king is to rejoice in the days of their youth. This means to "take advantage of" youth as a period of preparation. One of the three great decisions made by young people concerns their choice of vocation. In this day when the world is more specialized than ever before, young people are forced to make decisions on life's occupation earlier. The young person who sets himself against study, rebels against the authority of classroom, and refuses the discipline involved in the development of the mind is thwarted for the rest of his days because he did not "take advantage of" the days of his youth for preparation to live and serve.

Martin Luther set down the Protestant idea of every job

being a "divine calling." This means that a ditchdigger, schoolteacher, secretary, salesman, or physician is just as much entered into a calling of God as is the minister who preaches behind the pulpit on Sundays. To the Christian young person no job is just employment for money. It is a means for glorifying God through the dignity of hard work. If you intend to be a ditchdigger, farmer, minister, or teacher, then be the very best ditchdigger, farmer, minister, or teacher you possibly can be. This fulfillment of your life's vocation is a part of total Christian service. Whatever you do, do to the glory of God!

The second directive of the wise old king to young people is to "remove sorrow . . . and put away evil" from their lives. The second great decision which is made by young people concerns their choice of a life's companion. There is no more certain way to put sorrow into your heart or bring evil into your life for the rest of your days on earth than irresponsible behavior concerning dating and courtship. Someone has said that the three Rs for dating and courtship among teenagers are (1) respect for each other, (2) responsibility, and (3) restraint. Young people who fail to have respect, responsibility, and restraint get involved in serious behavior that results in heartache, remorse, and demoralizing guilt. This is why the ancient king advised, "Remove sorrow from thy heart, and put away evil."

The last directive of the king is "remember now thy Creator in the days of thy youth." It is during youth that final decisions are made on a system of values, a philosophy of life, a religious outlook, and even conversion to Jesus Christ as Lord and Master of life. Remember, God loves you and has a plan for your life. It is not by accident that you are in the world as you are today. His purpose is to fulfill your life as He has planned it. However, the one factor which disrupts all else in the development of a person's life is sin. When sin breaks the fellowship between a young person and the Spirit of God in the world, there is only one way of redemption and this is forgiveness through Jesus Christ. A life committed to Him in the days of youth will bear the fruits of "love, joy, peace, longsuffering, gentleness, goodness, faith, meekness, temperance: against such there is no law" (Gal. 5:22-23).

OSCAR F. REED is professor of preaching at Nazarene Theological Seminary. Prior to this assignment he taught at Pasadena College as chairman of the Division of Religion and Philosophy and at Bethany Nazarene College as the head of the Department of Religion. He has also taught at Syracuse University and at Pasadena City College.

For 15 years Dr. Reed pastored congregations in New England, Florida, California, and western Canada. He holds the A.B. and Th.B. degrees from Bethany Nazarene College and the M.Th. and Ph.D. degrees from the University of Southern California.

He is in demand across the nation as a convention speaker and revivalist. But his heart has always been in the pastoral ministry, and he delights in working with the scores of young men who come under his instruction.

NATIONAL HOLIDAYS

Oscar F. Reed

It is not my intention that these sermons prepared for "national occasions" should be delivered as they are, although I am not adverse to that. Anything that a teacher-preacher speaks or writes is open to use, perusal, criticism, and reorganization. As C. H. Spurgeon remarked, "But as the young prophet borrowed an ax of a friend, and was not censured for it so long as the strokes he gave it were his own, so may we refrain from condemning those who find a theme suggested to them, and a line of thought laid before them, and with all their hearts use them in speaking to the people" (*Sermon Notes*, 1888). I am reminded of what Samuel Young once said: "I always read books written by preachers, knowing that there is little profit in the writing. They must be telling the truth."

In my mind, pastoral preaching at special occasions is the most difficult to prepare. For one thing, there is only so much to be said. Second, the pattern is usually thematic (topical) and tends to intrude into the pastoral preaching mood.

On the other hand, festival occasions of the nation and Christian calendar break the rhythm of preaching and introduce subjects which are current, challenging, and I hope interesting.

Sermons on the four national holidays selected give the preacher an opportunity to work with obscure and interesting texts, history, literature, and current events. They also give access to preaching on the relation of the church and the fundamentals of the faith to vital community interests. While the nature of the sermon will, for the most part, be thematic, the pastor can use his skills of inference and illustration to make the text meaningful in the context it is given. The messages will be deeply appreciated and acted upon.

The four following sermons are of that nature. I have borrowed when borrowing enriched the material. But through exegesis and homiletical development I have tried to suggest four themes that might be helpful on these occasions. Use your own "ax" and make them appropriate for your fellowship.

William Stidger, a superb preacher of a former era, observed that there is no need to apologize for using the ideas of others so long as those ideas are touched by the "fire and form of the personality of the man who uses them. That is the genius of originality and has been in all lands and through all times in the creative world."

It is in this regard that the preacher who communicates the great thoughts of others (and are there any other?) speaks to those who hear them for the first time.

The Risen Christ—Memorial Day Promise

Scripture: John 20:14-16

Text: *Jesus saith unto her, Mary. She turned herself, and saith unto him, . . . Master* (John 20:16).

The meaning of Memorial Day has changed in recent years. It was first started in memory of soldiers who fought and died for the union of free people on the bloody battlefields of the Civil War. It was only after World War I, however, that we began to think of Memorial Day as a day for remembering all those who had given their lives for America. Today, Memorial Day is set aside in memory of all loved ones. Flowers cover the cemeteries as expressions of love and gratefulness. Memories are rich with meaning.

This Memorial Sunday brought my mind to another grave, a meeting, and one of the most intriguing events of Easter morning. It is a promise to all those who have lost loved ones—even the risen Christ.

It was in the dark and chill of early morning that Mary cried: "They have taken away my Lord, and I know not where they have laid him" (John 20:13). What sorrow! It reflects the cry of many human hearts deprived of the one they most prize and hold most dear.

It was after she had spoken these words that Mary saw in the shadows of the place a figure which she thought to be the gardener.

Mary said unto him, "Sir, if you have carried him away, tell me where you have laid him, and I will take him away" (John 20:15, RSV). Instead of answering her question, Jesus spoke only one word—"Mary."

Can you imagine what that meant to her? She had

heard her name in the darkness of the garden, and her sorrow turned to joy. Why shouldn't it? This same Jesus who had claimed Mary's love and loyalty and redeemed her life from the muddle of sin now stood outside the grave alive and well.

There were others who were far more reputable to whom Jesus might have revealed himself first. But He identified himself first to this "deep-feeling, lonely woman" whose memories spoke of reconciliation and redemption.

On this Memorial Sunday as we think of that moment when Mary first heard that voice, don't we more fully understand what the risen Christ means to human life?

I. The Risen Christ Is Not Remote from Us but as Close as Our Question and His Answer.

There are many of us who really look upon Christ as so far beyond us and above us that His world and our world never touch. We think of Him in celebration as having nothing to do with our dusty ways. He has become an ecclesiastical Christ who rests conveniently in a beautiful stained-glass window. But that is not the report that Mary brought to the disciples. "I have seen the Lord." She talked about One she had seen, who was as real as she was. One who was alive and filled with a sense of compassion and love—"alert to human need."

II. The Risen Christ Was Active Rather than Passive.

His resurrection meant a radical change for His followers. He invited them, as He does us, to take a genuine risk with Him. From that moment on He invited His disciples to keep their ear to the ground and discover human need. When we worship this risen Christ, the very one who spoke to Mary, we are saved from self-deception and are alive to the concerns of those who need to hear their name spoken by Jesus.

If we could really recover that living conviction of a risen Christ, do you believe that an evil society could stop Christ's Church? How many would rally to the cause if they really heard His voice speaking their name?

When men discover that Christ is alive, there is no room for indifference and halfheartedness. They find that His touch still holds its ancient power in a great tide of hope and enthusiasm. When we really believe that Christ is alive, the great potential of the Christian community becomes alive with hope and faith.

III. I Am Also Impressed that Mary Mistook Jesus for a Gardener.

Gardeners are those whose hands make plants grow. If Mary had to mistake Jesus for anyone else than who He was, it was significant that she should see Him as one who was forever creating and making things new. Christ was always close to nature. He knew the secrets of the fertile land, the rain that falls "on the just and on the unjust" (Matt. 5:45), the winds, the waves, and the sunsets. He was not offended when Mary looked upon Him as a gardener.

The revelation of Christ alive comes to many in stages as it did to Mary. We may at first mistake Christ for the gardener. Youth around the world, sensitive to the voice of the Master, are slowly awakening to the creative powers of a living Christ.

Many of us mistake the risen Christ for the gardener. The divine revelation is much richer than that. This Memorial Sunday ought to say that to us. You who grieve in the memory of those gone before can move from the shadows into the blazing light and hear the ring of His voice.

IV. There Is a Message to Those Who This Year Have Lost One Whom You Loved Dearly.

The depth of grief is known to many of you this morning. It is like Mary's grief when she came that early morning to Jesus' tomb. The darkness of that early morning is matched by the blazing light of Christian faith in a living Christ. Mary found that the ashes of her life were turned to blazing joy—and you too shall find the pain of separation turned to gladness.

When I go outside of Kansas City to Greenlawn Cemetery to visit my father's grave, I do not think of a disembodied memory. My mind relives the vibrant person he was—handsome, tall, talented, squared jaw, and squared shoulders. He was interested in my playing basketball, hollering with a crowd at a high school track meet or football game—vitally interested in his children. I cannot cast him into nameless oblivion. Actually, he lives again as a real friend and father.

What a waste it would be if the person of Jesus was a mystical ideal lost in the annals of history. No, He appears as a real, living reality—a friend who is here to answer our questions of disappointment with the name—"John," "Mary," "George," "Aletha," "Grace." And then we answer, "Master!"

As you go this afternoon to honor your loved ones with flowers, go with the spirit that there is One who is alive— a Memorial Day Promise.

A Word to the Nation

(July 4th)

Scripture: Exod. 3:7-15

Text: Exod. 3:13-14, RSV: *Then Moses said to God, "If I come to the people of Israel and say to them, 'The God of your fathers has sent me to you,' and they ask me, 'What is his name?' what shall I say to them?" God said to Moses, "I am who I am." And he said, "Say this to the people of Israel, 'I am has sent me to you.' "*

Every man stands astride three generations: the one before, the one after, and the one of which he is a member. World War II and the succeeding political, social, and economic issues have changed all of that. The nation stands where tradition means very little and the future is unknown.

Five men, among others, have molded our society: Charles Darwin, Karl Marx, Albert Einstein, John Dewey, and Sigmund Freud. Not a one confessed to be a Christian in the evangelical sense. The result is a perspective which is secular—a reference which is man-centered rather than God-centered.

Out of this comes one central question that is important:

Does God reveal himself today as our forefathers witnessed, and if so, how?

If He doesn't, then we are on our own—in a meaningless universe which is no more than what we make of it. And many feel this way! If, however, God does reveal himself, then we who are Christ's disciples must learn how to communicate how He does, and what that revelation means for our nation here and now!

The story of Moses at the burning bush and the revelation of God to him, I believe, helps us to answer the question.

Names were important in Old Testament times. Abram meant "exalted father." Abraham meant the "father of many nations." The name Naomi meant happy, lovely, and beautiful.

The king always had two names: the first by which he was known, and a secret name which revealed his character and essence. To know his secret name was to hold power over him.

The God of Abraham, Isaac, and Jacob responded to Moses' question by revealing the name which most perfectly represented His character. Moses had the audacity to ask, "What is your name?" (v. 13) and more astounding, God answered with a name: "I AM THAT I AM"!

That name in the Hebrew (Yahweh) was a name so sacred that it could neither be uttered or written, so the Hebrews replaced it with "Lord" (Adonai) which the early Christians used to identify our Savior (Kurios). That sacred name given to Moses represents the rallying call of a new nation: "I AM," "I SHALL BECOME," "I SHALL BECOME TO YOU."

He was saying to Moses: The God of creation is entering into your experience to give you leadership, to triumph when you triumph, to suffer when you suffer, and to follow you down through your history to exile and return. I am your God. "I shall become to you."

But does that say anything to us? Can we contemporize the experience to our nation?

I. God Revealed Himself Most Authentically in the Time of His People's Greatest Need (v. 7).

The Hebrews had suffered slavery for 400 years. They were under the strong hand of a king "which knew not

Joseph" (1:8). Their God seemed far away in another country. There was no hope or future.

Victor Frankl, the German psychiatrist, tells how in World War II, when he had lost his possessions, friends, and loved ones to the tyranny of the Nazis, he finally stood naked in the snow before his tempters. Later he recounted, "I can't understand how I endured the shame and deprivation. But then came a wonderful faith that after all I had suffered—there was nothing to fear except my Heavenly Father."

Our nation stands this day in a time of desperate need. It is during these times that God can reveal himself most authentically. "I shall become to you."

II. God Revealed Himself Most Authentically in the Face of His Chosen Leader's Insecurities (v. 11).

Moses replied to God's charge, "Who am I that I should go to Pharaoh . . . ?" (RSV). He felt insufficient and inadequate for the task. He was a different man from the young son of the princess and the heir to the throne who had arrogantly slain the Egyptian.

I was called to the home of an affluent businessman who in one evening had lost a million dollars and stood penniless with very little future in sight. He did not know which way to turn. The strength of yesterday was now the weakness of today. I knew only one way to turn—and he turned with me. It is in these times that God begins to speak. Before, Moses could not because of his own self-sufficiency, but in the loss of all, he now heard another voice, "I shall become to you."

The 80s are years in which we have had very little direction and a great deal of confusion. Perhaps now is the time to listen once again to His name, "I shall become to you."

III. God Revealed Himself Most Authentically When He Confronted Moses Through His Word.

"And the Lord said" (v. 7). He, the "Holy One of Israel," united himself to His chosen people by *acting* and *saying*, "I shall become to you."

We need this word on our national birthday. If God spoke words of assurance to Israel through Moses, He can speak again to us if we will respond by accepting Him as our God through His Son, Jesus Christ. That assurance was deliberately wrapped up in His name, Yahweh, I AM THAT I AM—I will become to you.

It has always been that way—God uses great words to speak to our anxieties. Ordinarily, they are identified with His name.

Isaiah knew this when he represented the Lord saying (43:2-3, RSV):

"When you pass through the waters I will be with you;
    and through the rivers, they shall not overwhelm you;
when you walk through fire you shall not be burned,
    and the flame shall not consume you.
For I am the Lord your God,
    the Holy One of Israel, your Savior."

As Israel journeyed with the Lord down through the years, His promise "to become with" is fulfilled in a context so deep and profound that in the end it involves the actual entry of God himself into the life of man—even our Lord and Christ.

My message could be one of despair and discouragement, but for the Christian it is one of hope! The condition for that hope is found in 2 Chron. 7:14.

"If my people who are called by my name humble themselves, and pray and seek my face, and turn from their wicked ways, then I will hear from heaven, and will forgive their sin and heal their land" (RSV).

The promise was given nearly 1,400 years before the

Advent when God said, as He says to our nation this morning, "Tell them My name is YAHWEH—I will become to you."

God's Word on This Labor Day

Scripture: Mic. 6:1-8

Text: Mic. 6:8: *He hath shewed thee, O man, what is good; and what doth the Lord require of thee, but to do justly, and to love mercy, and to walk humbly with thy God?*

What has the church to say today concerning the vocation of labor and the issues of labor in our nation? It is easy to say nothing, to be dumb, to ignore the situation and go on preaching the "simple gospel." That is what some of the brethren advise.

But what is the "simple gospel"? Is it a corpse? Has it nothing to do with real life? John the Baptist did not think so. When the people came to him and asked: "What shall we do?" someone might have said to him: "Do not be too specific; just preach the simple gospel." But John was very specific, and said: "He who has two coats, let him share with him who has none; and he who has food, let him do likewise" (Luke 3:11, RSV). When the soldiers came and asked: "What shall we do?" someone might have said: "John, don't get personal, just preach the simple gospel." But John thrust to the heart of the matter and said: "Rob no one by violence or by false accusation, and be content with your wages" (v. 14, RSV). He told the tax collectors to take no more than was due and told Herod to straighten out his life morally. There is no evasion in the "simple gospel." The religion that speaks not to real issues is a sham. The church must speak clearly, coherently, and scripturally to the issues that face our nation in the 80s.

The church is the one agent that must bring both capital and labor under the judgment of God, and calmly, yet clearly, attempt to interpret to men the teachings of the Bible on questions which today rend our society.

There are two facts which the Bible addresses:

I. The First of These Is the Vocation of Labor.

Nowhere in the Scriptures can one discover any position other than an emphasis on the dignity of labor.

God is on the side of the worker. He has rights; the idle has none, whether he belongs to the idle rich or the idle poor. "If any one will not work, let him not eat" (2 Thess. 3:10, RSV). This is the most primitive of rights—the right to keep from starving. One cannot read the Bible without seeing over and over again how God was (and is) on the side of the underprivileged.

On the other hand, the privilege of that promise was to those who gave themselves to labors. I can see where the initial motive of the federal and state welfare programs was well taken. But it has become a monster, supporting those who need no support or those who are not willing to work.

However, the Bible definition of work is not confined to manual labor. The most difficult work is that work of the brain, soul, and self as well as hands. Actually, the man whose hands are not guided by a well-disciplined mind must remain mediocre.

Workingmen do not need our sympathy. The greatest tragedy that I can imagine is to see a man who has nothing to do.

It is in this regard that church and state must join hands in providing work for any man or woman who desires to work. A nation which does not create through labor is on the road to oblivion.

II. The Bible Also Teaches that Ownership Is Sacred, Both Private and Public.

God commands, "Hands off your neighbor's property." What one owns is his. If not, the Ten Commandments would not have said, "You shall not steal" (Exod. 20:15, RSV). There were exacting penalties in the Old Testament for those who took what was not theirs. The work of the anarchist who destroys property in what he believes to be "the interests of the people" is actually destroying himself. Ownership is sacred, and the man who wantonly destroys his neighbor's property registers himself as an outlaw. I understand, I believe, the frustration of the poor and the blacks of Miami and Brooklyn. But is there no other way to express that frustration than through destruction and violence?

The other side of the coin suggests that ownership is a trust as well as a right. No one has a right to hoard, or profiteer, or even use his property for himself. Property is a trust, and we are stewards.

It is in this spirit that capital must remember that God lives with the man who works, and labor must not violate private trust.

These two principles have been foundational to democratic tradition. They cannot be ignored without destroying what we have treasured for over 200 years. We must recognize the dignity and rights of labor on the one hand, and the sanctity of ownership on the other.

III. Our Text Shows the Church Has a Threefold Message to the Nation on This Labor Day.

"He has showed you, O man, what is good; and what does the Lord require of you" (RSV):

A. *"To be just"* (Moffatt)

God is concerned with *being* prior to *doing*. The

113

question is not how much a man is worth, but what kind of a man is he, and what is his life? The only line that God draws between men is whether they are what they confess to be. Both the unscrupulous poor who plunders and pillages and the rich who oppresses and exploits are under judgment. The selfish millionaire and the bum who throws a bomb are in the same class. God's first condition is to "do justly."

Justice means equity to the laboring man. Thus, the employer who does not give a just wage is exploiting the laborer. Labor is not committing treason when it attempts to better its lot in life through legitimate and lawful means. The question of wages and life supports will never be settled properly until justice holds the scales.

Justice also means a square deal for capital. The owner must not be looked upon as a foe of humanity if he makes a *fair* profit and chooses to exercise certain rights which are his by definition. He, too, is entitled to justice. Labor will never help itself by wronging its employer.

Justice is the reign of law. Law is a man's only protection.

The church would say to our people today, "Do justly." Only in this spirit can we hope to build a better order.

B. *"To love kindness"* (RSV)

The Authorized Version has translated the phrase, "to love mercy." Justice must be tempered by mercy or "loving-kindness."

Our nation needs a baptism of good will through God's grace. It cries for a perspective which says that we shall see the good in others as well as the bad—a point of view which seeks men out of love rather than hate.

Gene Outka in *Agape* has suggested that the love that is required is a love of "other-regard" which is concerned

114

about the other *just because he is there*. Without it, all of our laws fall short of a cure.

"What does the Lord require of you . . . ?"—justice in the context of loving-kindness. He insists that we shall be as profoundly interested in others as we are in ourselves. Our Heavenly Father does not desire mercy for expedience, but because mercy will tear down barriers and make men brethren. No wonder Jesus said, "Blessed are the merciful, for they shall obtain mercy" (Matt. 5:7).

C. *"To walk humbly with your God"* (RSV)

Our relation to our God is prior to either justice or loving-kindness. The climax of God's triple command is in a right relationship with Him.

Labor will never be just to capital as long as it is wrong with God. Capital will never be merciful to labor as long as it is wrong with God. The will of God always comes first, and we cannot hope to build a Christian social order until we put God first.

Fifty years ago Dr. James I. Vance, in speaking of labor relations in America, said that the issues would only change when we take the matters that separate us into His presence. If it was true in 1930, how much more important it is in 1980.

His challenge then was as is mine now: The greatest things in life are not wages and profits, but character.

Our deepest need is God, and no man's plight is so desperate as the one who is without God.

A Word to All of Us on Veterans Day

SCRIPTURE: Judg. 7:19—8:2

TEXT: Judg. 8:2: *And he said unto them, What have I done now in comparison of you? Is not the gleaning of the grapes of Ephraim better than the vintage of Abiezer?*

It would seem at first that this passage from Judges is not compatible with the day that we celebrate—Veterans Day. A second look, however, may speak to us of an ancient event that is really current in its implications.

The text, "Is not the gleaning of the grapes of Ephraim better than the vintage of Abiezer?" was a gracious and beautiful reply which Gideon made to the bold, cold-blooded Ephraimites. The victory represented a great day for Israel. The trumpet, the pitcher, and the lamp had led to a great victory for Gideon's "three hundred."

The men of Midian did not know who attacked them as the army of Israel dropped out of the night. Then, after the battle was over, the Ephraimites were called into the fray. They could now gather the fruit that another had shaken from the tree. They could shout the song of victory that others had earned—and instead of appreciation, Gideon drew only criticism. Ungrateful, ungenerous, querulous because they were not called to battle, they loaded Gideon with abuses.

It is a marvel that Gideon answered as he did. If ever there is a time when criticism is mean, it is when others have just come in from doing their duty.

Yet, Gideon had a gracious word for them. He had fought in order that others might enjoy the spoils of his victory. His was the weariness, pain, and sacrifice; theirs was the comfort, the spoil, and the gain. "Is not the gleaning of the grapes of Ephraim better than the vintage of Abiezer?''

This, then, is our Veterans Day proclamation. There are those in our midst who represent Gideon's 300. They have soaked the fields of Flanders, the mountains of Korea, and the jungles of Vietnam with their blood. And we are rich because they dared to fight for their country. We have entered into an inheritance of peace because of their agony.

Well I know that there are questions about the viability of any war, the motives for fighting, and the subtle conflicts in our own nation over the fighting. But for now, this is the day to demonstrate a note of deep appreciation for what others have done in our name.

We are, for the most part, like the Ephraimites who came on later to follow the flag rather than to hold it in battle. It is the old picture of Ephraim and Abiezer reproduced.

I. I Am Impressed that the Same Picture Is Reproduced Today.

We have never learned to be as generous as we should be to those men who represented us. I am well aware of the soul-tearing issues that racked our nation over Vietnam. I am confident that thousands who returned from the jungles came home with mixed emotions. But we, in our securities, owe them something. We need to be thoroughly generous to those who risked their lives for us. Ours is an immortal debt that can never be overpaid. Let it not be said that we are perennially ungrateful.

II. Another Observation That Might Be Made Is that Gideon's Men Fought Not for Themselves.

They went forth for the sake of Israel. The spoil that they won for themselves was not a tithe of what they secured for their nation. Their victory represented a heritage for generations yet unborn. They were struggles for the future. That made their fame secure.

Motive makes the difference on whether a war is just. There is nothing beautiful or meaningful about two ruffians pummeling each other. But I have known a man to defend a woman's honor or support a child in which his blows were not blameworthy, but honorable.

Whether any war in our world context can be just, I know not. But one thing is certain: We should express our deep commendation to those who in the call of a nation fought not for themselves, but for wives, sweethearts, mothers, and dads who represented the best that they wanted conserved at home.

III. But the Function of Veterans Day Is Twofold.

If it expresses a generous appreciation for both the living and dead who have served their country, it ought also to have an exhortation for those who have not served in active duty.

A. We must see in our day what the Ephraimites did not express in theirs—magnanimity. We may not agree with our nation's actions or its leaders' goals, but we must not withhold our generosity from those who have given of themselves in service.

I can remember the cheers, tears, and hilarity when our men came back from Korea and Japan. I cannot get away from the embarrassed silence we gave to our veterans from Vietnam. They, too, are of the corps. They, too, were in the mire of field and the danger of jungle. Is it our pride that holds back our magnanimity? Let us take this day to say one big "thank-you" in defeat as well as victory and tell all our men that we are one with them in their sacrifice for us.

B. One last item must come to us in strong truth. The

118

men of Gideon had given themselves in sacrifice. *Self-sacrifice* is that cathartic which makes it possible to move from where we are to where we want to go. Self-sacrifice includes not only the veterans we honor, but those among us who honor them.

In Scotland there is a battlefield on which the Scots and Saxons met in terrible encounter. There is no monument to mark the spot, but a singular, little blue flower grows there alone. They call it the "flower of Culloden" because it sprung from the soil in which the bodies of patriots were buried. The seeds needed the baptism of blood to make them grow. The field is memorialized today by every blue flower that represents brave men who gave their lives for others.

Dear friends, the choicest flowers are always "Culloden" flowers. They spring from the soil of sacrifice. The kingdom of God is made up of that kind of self-sacrifice. It is not easy to be a disciple of Jesus. It takes more than an easy nod or slight approval. The Kingdom is made up of those who find that authentic Christians always suffer at some time or other. No man is a real citizen of the Kingdom until he has opened his veins for another—even Jesus Christ.

Obedience, magnanimity, self-sacrifice. This is the trinity of patriotic graces that Veterans Day must teach us.

JARRELL W. GARSEE is pastor of the First Church of the Nazarene of Boise, Ida., where he has served since 1976. A graduate of Bethany Nazarene College and Nazarene Theological Seminary, he also holds an M.S. degree from Oklahoma University and the Ph.D. in developmental psychology from Ohio State University.

His career has included pastoring in Texas, missionary service in Samoa from 1960 to 1968, and director of counseling services and professor of behavioral sciences at Mount Vernon Nazarene College from 1968 to 1976. A member of the National Honor Society and the American Psychological Association, Dr. Garsee authored *Samoa Diary* and has contributed to various church periodicals.

FAMILY

Jarrell W. Garsee

The joy of sharing the *exciting*, life-changing gospel is heightened by those occasions when loving relationships may be exposed for eternal glory.

My own concern for ministry in these days is determined by these major beliefs:

1. *Love is the most enduring factor of God's great creation.* Jesus' greatest commandment was twofold: "Thou shalt love . . . God . . . [and] thy neighbour" (Matt. 22: 36-40). The greatest . . . is love!

2. *Home and family provide opportunities of great potential, for either heartaches or fulfillment, in these primary relationships.* What happens between the people who belong to one another plays a greater role in determining eternal investments and eternal destiny than nearly any other force.

3. *Only Christ's intervening love ("the Good News") can redeem human relationships from selfishness and sin to make them ideally blessed and a blessing.* Apart from the "divine interference" ("The Word becoming flesh and sharing our lives"), our closest human love can be colored by control, coercion, and resistance.

4. *Those occasions when hearts are already tuned to think of home and family can be used by the Holy Spirit to "intrude with grace."* The emotions can be joined to the mind and the will by proclamation in the power of the Spirit, and lives and relationships can be changed.

121

Any of the holy days, or holidays, that bring families together are good. Some of the appropriate occasions for such emphasis include
—Family Altar Sunday—January
—National Family Week—May
—National Baby Day—May
—Mother's Day—May
—Father's Day—June
—Children's Day—July
—Grandparent's Day—September
—Thanksgiving—November
—Christmas—December

The goal for such messages and services is to
—encourage appreciation
—engender consideration
—provide scriptural basis for growth
—give opportunity for commitment
—emphasize God's power to renew broken relationships
—share the truth of the Spirit's strength for super-human (spiritual) victory in difficult relationships
—remind of the unbelievable power of God's "first-move," initiating love
—confirm new directions and new dynamics for ministering to one another in their first-line relationships

God's Plan for the Family

(Family Altar Sunday)

SCRIPTURE: Deut. 6:1-9

God's plan for people is wholeness. His place for producing this wholeness is in the succeeding generations of godly people within the home.

One of the basic needs for maximizing spiritual nurture in the home is to recognize the wholeness of the environment. We often seem to think of injecting some spiritual nourishment into a person's atmosphere, rather than allowing that person to live in a total atmosphere characterized by spiritual reality. In the Old Testament, this total atmospheric absorption is verbalized in Deut. 6:1-9. Listen to a few of those phrases: "Love him with *all* your heart, soul, and might. . . . think constantly about these commandments . . . teach them to your children and talk about them . . . at home or out for a walk; at bedtime and the first thing in the morning" (vv. 5-7, TLB). To view religious instruction as part of spiritual nurture or to compartmentalize religious instruction is to destroy the basis for spiritual nurture.

Let's think plainly about a few potential problem areas that can affect the environment:

A. Some relegate God to a specific day, time, or activity level without allowing Him to be the Lord of their entire lives.

B. Children are sent to church for spiritual nurture rather than being taken in a loving, involved family unit.

C. God's Word, God's name, and God's cause have no meaningful part in conversations or community life other than at certain, separate times.

123

D. The moral-ethical standards of God and His Word are not applied to the actual everyday operation of monetary transactions and decision-making.

E. The power of God's forgiving love is not allowed to flow into the personal relationships of the home in healing, blessing, renewing power.

I. Listen Well!

Twice in this scripture we are reminded to hear (vv. 3 and 4) the vital truth that there is only one God, He is Lord, and we will do well to obey Him!

Even our hearts should hear (v. 5). It takes time—reading, memorizing, quoting, meditating, sharing, praying, hearing—to really listen with our whole being to the deeper realities beneath the "tense temporaries" of our lives.

Listen, also, well to the heart cries of individual family members. Be sensitive to the times when they need to receive spiritual encouragement!

II. Love Wisely!

Every generation (v. 2)—father, son, and son's son—must redetermine to place God as the highest object of affection.

These personal, positive values must be transmitted by example. Love is not taught; it is learned by heart!

The little boy who came home from Sunday School and reported that his Sunday School teacher was Jesus' grandmother astounded his family. But when they asked him why he said that, he answered, "Because she wouldn't talk about anyone else, and she kept showing us His picture." Then they knew—his teacher loved wisely from a whole heart!

Let that love flow from one family member to another.

Do not allow sibling rivalry to dictate the emotional climate of the home. One family that I know has the "loving rule" that each day each member of the family must say, "I love you," out loud to each other member of the family. They declare that they can tell by the change in the atmosphere if someone stops loving in word or in deed.

III. Labor Worthily!

Teaching God's Word and commandments and statutes is a full-time job (v. 7). It must not be an afterthought or an insertion into an already crowded schedule. You reveal God's will while you're sitting at home, when you're walking together, while you're resting, and at the beginning of the day!

The whole operation and organization of the family should be saturated with consistent examples of forgiving, rejoicing, interceding, praising, praying, honesty, vulnerability, faith, patience, and hard work, or at least creative persistence in maintaining the reality of spiritual life!

What you are, what you believe, and what you hope are the major labors of the faithful revealer of God's love.

In closing, I want to share with you two portions of scripture, in a very free paraphrase, and a statement with which I agree, which summarizes this topic.

"Teach your child how and why to choose the right path, and when he gets older, he will keep on choosing it for himself" (Prov. 22:6).

Please note that it very specifically does not say to choose the right path for your child!

"Quietly trust yourself to Christ your Lord, and if anybody [even your own child] asks why you believe as you do, be ready to tell him, and do it in a gentle and respectful way" (1 Pet. 3:15).

These words from Paul C. Payne are an appropriate summary:

> Having a Christian home means far more than having a houseful of nice people who treat each other fairly kindly and who go to church fairly regularly. It means a home where Christ is known and loved and served; where children come to know Him through their parents; where the Christian training of the children is put ahead of the social ambition of the father; where the father is determined to carry on his business in conformity with the mind of Christ; where both father and mother are determined to make their social life conform to high Christian ideals; and where eyes see far horizons of a world to be won for Christ.[1]

Husbands, Love Your Wives

(Christian Marriage)

SCRIPTURE: Eph. 5:15-33

The disengagement of so many men from the emotional and spiritual leadership in their homes is humorously illustrated by a story of the "man who watches" in the book by H. Page Williams, *Do Yourself a Favor: Love Your Wife!*

The *macho* image, the egoistic concerns, and the press of economic and cultural demands render so many men unwilling to "lead in love." Christ comes as the supreme Example and enables to help the godly man take authority in the marriage relationship, an authority based not on power and privilege but on sacrifice and service.

---

1. Paul S. Rees, *Christian: Commit Yourself* (Old Tappan, N.J.: Fleming H. Revell Co., 1957), pp. 91-92.

I. Like Christ, the Husband Is to Love.

The man must care for and be attentive to the needs of his wife. He must provide opportunity for warm, intimate sharing emotionally. Dr. James Dobson, in *What Wives Wish Their Husbands Knew About Women*, reveals that poor self-esteem growing out of absence of communication is one of a woman's greatest problems. A husband must gratify the needs of his wife, not serve his own ends.

II. Like Christ, the Husband Must Sacrifice for His Wife.

As the husband gives away his own rights, freedoms, and pride, he *must* utilize the radical grace of the cross of Jesus Christ. He forgives, tearing up "due notes" from the past, and gives himself up to provide a motivational environment in which the wife can follow both her husband and her Savior.

III. Like Christ, the Husband Gives Spiritual Leadership.

The cleansing, the proper use of talents, the act of setting his wife apart for "wholeness" and godly service must be the concern of her husband. The husband "purifies" his family by leading them in healthy, joyful pursuits that re-create, create, and give opportunity for *growth*, especially spiritually.

IV. Like Christ, the Husband Guards His Wife.

The man sees to it that no unnecessary strain or drain is placed upon his wife, especially not by his own default or failure! He stands between her and difficulty—financially, physically, emotionally. He provides for her basic needs and protects her from the world so that she may "shine gloriously" in "wholeness."

V. Like Christ, the Husband Directs the Wife.

Never should a man use dictatorial terms, but direct in submission first to Christ, and then in loving, God-directed, choices of priorities. He must discern God's will for his family, point the direction in love, and then prayerfully seek God's dynamic and timing for the process of ministering together in God's world.

Christ loved and gave himself! As the Christian husband follows that example, God's grace infills and fulfills these special family relationships.

Commit today to follow Him in His example of unselfish love!

A Mother's Commitment

(Mother's Day)

SCRIPTURE: 1 Samuel 1 and 2

God's people were living in troubled times. They needed a man who would give them a new glimpse of God's power and presence. As He so often does, God began to provide that man by a mother's commitment.

I. Hannah Was Committed to God.

Before she was a mother, Hannah was godly. Before she was a wife, she was a believer and worshipper.

She believed in prayer, in open, honest communication with God (1:10). Her prayer was rooted in the will of God: "if thou wilt" (1:11). Her prayer was earnest and sincere, and she linked herself to God by a difficult vow. Even when she was openly criticized and accused falsely by the priest on duty who mistook her deeply felt prayer for drunkenness, she did not become defensive. She was polite and vulnerable, but persuasive.

Hannah held a vital, personal, first-name basis of relationship with God. Nothing could move her away from that commitment.

II. Hannah Was Committed to Her Husband.

Before she was a mother, Hannah was a loving, obedient wife. She did this in difficult circumstances. She was not her husband's only wife (1:2). She was barren and had no children (1:2). Her sister-wife criticized her and provoked her so that she was sad (1:6). But she refused to bear tales to her husband even when her husband asked the cause of her sadness (1:8). Instead, she forgave the other wife, committed herself in unselfish love to her husband Elkanah, and prayed to God. She poured out her grief before the Lord, and not bitterness upon the others in her household.

III. Hannah Was Committed to Her Children.

The family came late, and she was undoubtedly tempted to cling to the first, especially, because of this; but she wanted the best for them, and that meant obedience to God's will and to her vow.

A. In the first child's name, Samuel, she acknowledged that she had asked him of the Lord (1:20).

B. She provided early spiritual training, until formal "weaning" (not only physical but emotional), probably age seven.

C. She made the spiritual sacrifice of bringing him to the house of the Lord, while "the child was young" (1:24).

D. She *joyfully* relinquished him to the Lord, and sang a powerful hymn of praise about her faith (2:1-10).

E. She was given glorious fulfillment: five more children.

F. She continued to minister in prayer and care for Samuel, seeing him every year with a new garment and assurance of her continuing commitment.

Hannah:

　　—Getting her commitments right
　　　—keeping her spirit straight
　　　　—holding her purpose firm
　　　　　—proving her priorities aligned

provided the source through which God provided a great *fulfillment*

　　—for Elkanah, her husband
　　　—for Samuel and her other children
　　　　—for the other wife in her home
　　　　　—for her own life
　　　　　　—for God's nation
　　　　　　　—for *eternity!*

Honour Thy Father and Thy Mother

(Children's Sunday)

SCRIPTURE: Eph. 6:1-10

At least eight times, God's Word declares, "Honour thy father and thy mother":

—Exod. 20:12	—Matt. 19:19	—Luke 18:20
—Deut. 5:16	—Mark 7:10	—Eph. 6:2
—Matt. 15:4	—Mark 10:19	

Though we usually associate that particular commandment with the Old Testament, the truth is that six of the eight times it is repeated and stressed is in the New Testament.

It reveals a vital truth about the will of God for proper development in the home and family. Three basic principles are involved:

I. Parents, Be Honorable!

Love is not just an emotion or a feeling. It is quite evidently also an act of the will, for God commands us to love: "A new commandment I give unto you, That ye love" (John 13:34).

At the same time, trust and respect and the other half of love (mutual sharing) must be built upon *trustworthiness!*

Parents must earn the right to be trusted; they must gain the privilege of being respected; they must be honorable.

There are many negative things happening in some homes today:
—child abuse and neglect
—single-family care
—parents driven by materialism and ambition
—hostility and unresolved tensions
—time improperly used
—love sought but not given

Parents, it is your God-given privilege and responsibility to let God's love pour through you into the lives of your children, making you eternally honorable in their eyes and hearts!

II. Children, Honor Your Parents!

Honoring parents isn't automatic, even if parents are godly, unselfish, and dedicated. The Tempter and the temper of our times both predispose the hearts of children and young people to resist authority. This is one of the basic human (unredeemed) characteristics.

It has often been apparent to us when our own children have the greatest difficulty with resentment, resistance, or rebellion to parents, home, church, or God, it is because of unresolved spiritual tension in their own hearts.

Children must choose to *invite* Jesus Christ to come in as Lord and Savior of their own hearts. They must choose then to resist the heavy prevalence of disregard for parental concern so common around them. It is so easy to float into the peer group crowd's way of making fun of all the "old fogeys" of the parents' generation. Then children must choose to accept the fact that parents are human and therefore prone to mistakes, and they must choose to keep on giving them honor for their intentions if not for their actual intervention.

You see, *honoring* is also an active verb, based upon a willingness of spirit and a covenant relationship of committed love to one another and to God.

There's a bonus! Paul reminds us (in Eph. 6:2-3) that this is the "first commandment with promise." Honoring father and mother provides a peace and power for life that adds both quantity and quality to human existence—"it may be well with thee, and thou mayest live long."

In counseling, sometimes years after a parent has died, a child now grown physically but still retarded emotionally, will realize that unforgiving attitudes toward that parent, resentment and hostility (dishonoring) have created great difficulty in present relationships. The quality and probably even the length of life have been affected negatively by the refusal or failure to honor the father and mother. It takes God's miraculous inner-working grace to enable us to do this life-changing work of our will and heart!

III. Families, Honor God!

In the context in Ephesians, Paul reveals that good family relationships minister to Christ and provide strength.

One of the frightening things about our civilization today is the dissolution of the family. Death, desertion, divorce, disengagement, all contribute to the destruction of those ties needed to provide "the nurture and admonition of the Lord" (Eph. 6:4).

At the same time, the Holy Spirit is giving Christians new and dynamic tools for making their family a haven of peace from the world, a place to be strengthened, and a point from which to share Christ with their world.

The wise man said that "righteousness exalteth" (Prov. 14:34). Parents that purpose with God and children to be honorable, children who covenant with God and parents to be honoring, will build a source of honor to God, reestablishing the grace of Christ in their world.

The tremendous effect of parent-child relationships is underlined in Deut. 5:9-10. This scripture reveals that both iniquity and blessing are passed down from one generation to another. Honorable parents and honoring children will enable God to show "mercy unto thousands."

Children, your children and grandchildren will be among them!

ALAN L. RODDA is pastor of the First Church of the Nazarene, Portland, Ore., where he has served since 1972. He received his A.B. from Northwest Nazarene College; his B.D. from Nazarene Theological Seminary; and his Ph.D. from the Graduate Theological Union in Berkeley, Calif.

In addition to his pastoral experience in Washington, Kansas, California, and Oregon, Dr. Rodda served on the faculty of Northwest Nazarene College for three years; as a graduate fellow at the Pacific School of Religion; and now serves on the faculty of Warner Pacific College, and on the adjunct faculty of San Francisco Theological Seminary. He is a licensed therapist.

Under his pastoral leadership Portland First has experienced continued growth and a recent relocation to a newly completed church campus. In addition to numerous professional articles, he is a contributing author to *Human Development: A Holistic Approach* and *To the City with Love*.

COMMUNION

Alan L. Rodda

For I received from the Lord what I also delivered to you . . . For as often as you eat this bread and drink the cup, you proclaim the Lord's death until he comes (1 Cor. 11: 23, 26, RSV).

There is hardly a passage in the New Testament of more concern for the pastor, for it mandates him to perpetually continue one of the most sacred acts of worship in the church, the sacrament of the Lord's Supper.

Yet, this is an ordinance largely relegated to infrequent occurrence in the typical evangelical worship service. It is probably the "special day" syndrome which has reduced the practice of the sacrament to Holy Week and Worldwide Communion Sunday. While there is merit to making Communion special, it is too rich and potentially powerful an event in the worship of believers to diminish its occurrence and meaning.

In our church, Communion is both special and frequent. It is conducted at least 12 times a year as an integral part of the worship service. There is both a theological and experiential reason for that. If we really believe that the incarnation of Christ is not only a past event, but a present empowering reality, worship leaders must find ways to make this condescension of God into our lives, relationships, and situations both real and relevant. Through the repeated special use of the sacraments we help people discover the Cross as hope of forgiveness and the basis for living.

Communion is more than a performance of eating and drinking. It is now looked forward to as a vital way of appropriating God's resources for today and tomorrow's living. We do not need to fully understand the mysteries of the sacrament to teach our people to benefit from it, just as we do not need to understand the mysteries of digestion to be nourished by the food we eat. Our task, therefore, is to conduct the sacrament in such a way as to put people into living contact with Jesus Christ and create bridges between His redemption resources and their present needs.

This leads to a second personal philosophy about celebrating the sacrament. Since each person filters the sacrifice of Christ through his understanding of his own needs, the sacrament can never mean the same. Therefore, the worship leader must both communicate and conduct the ordinance in such a way to meet many personal and corporate needs. For example, in our large metropolitan area many of our people are desperately lonely. I have often, at a Communion service, arranged the congregation into small groups around the sanctuary, preinstructing lay leaders to make everyone acquainted with some key question and responses. Partaking of the element has then been shared in small clusters of people in a spirit of togetherness.

A variation of that is for small-group leaders to receive prayer requests around the circle and engage the group in burden-bearing prayer prior to the partaking of the bread and wine. Occasionally, I will challenge participants to go to another person, or couples to one another, in the service and ask for forgiveness, or extend affirmation and support. Following this experience, Communion will be shared together at the leader's instructions. Tying into various specific needs through the sacrament is an excellent way to complement those other instances in which the intention of the leader is to focus worshippers' attention exclusively onto the awesomeness of the cross of Christ.

Communion can also be an effective tool of evangelism. Many times I invite participants to confess sin and accept the atonement of Christ for their own lives. It is not biblically credible to view Paul's "partaking unworthily" passage as shutting out the person who is a sinner and who knows it to be so. This approach is never closed to the penitent sinner. Paul makes clear in the context (1 Cor. 11: 29) that eating and drinking unworthily refers to the people who either have no appreciation of the sanctity of the experience or who, with their divisiveness, hatred, or contemptuousness towards brothers or sisters, divide the church and are at variance with the others for whom Christ died. Many of our people have responded to the invitation and found peace with God by participating in the sacrament of Communion.

Methodologically, the Communion experience is an excellent way in which to practice the priesthood of all believers. While the serving of the elements by elders lends an often desired aura of pastoral impact to the experience, the serving of the elements by one layperson to another reinforces the total ministering body concept of the church. Nowhere in Scripture are elders exclusively mandated to serve the elements. Rather, the apostle Paul stresses the need for this experience to lend to total body unity and ministry. Often, rather than our elders, I will ask several laypersons of spiritual credibility to become the Communion leaders rather than our elders. The results, especially on the small-group level, have been electric, and the resulting sense of partnership with the pastor in ministry has been enhanced.

Communion needs to be both regular and special. The sacramental experience can meet a variety of needs and lend to Body life and leadership as well as point to the sacrifice of Christ. I encourage you to make this experience both sacred and healing to your people.

The Power of the Cross

SCRIPTURE: Rom. 5:1-11

I. Introduction

In these 11 short verses is revealed the heart of the living gospel. On a cross Christ died for our sins and brought us together with God. The symbol of our holy faith is the Cross. Moralists may find it offensive, sophisticates crude. But there can be no vital Christianity without a cross at the center. The true believer discerns in the Cross the wisdom and power of God, and the only hope of a world gone mad.

II. The Cross Event

Why this concentration on a cross? Let me suggest at least three facts that we should perceive as we contemplate the cross of Jesus Christ.

A. *A Victory Won*

To the citizens of that century, reference to a cross would have been more than startling; it would have been ridiculous. There was nothing wondrous about a cross. It was ugly, shameful, sordid, the fate reserved for the worst of criminal offenders. Cicero expressed the revulsion to the Cross when he wrote: "It is not only having to endure with a fate that is intolerable, it is also the mode of it, the anticipation, the very mention of it."

How then did this ugly thing become the glowing theme of our faith? Obviously, it was not the Cross but the Person who died on it. If it had not been for the Person, the Cross still would be a despised symbol of shame. God died on the Cross. God, in Christ, died on the Cross; and because of that, it has become a powerful symbol.

But it is more than God dying that makes the Cross so great. It is also God victorious over the death the Cross caused. The Christ who died on that Cross was not a pathetic victim, but a princely victor. In the Cross we see a victory won. Jesus did not go to the Cross pathetically broken as a condemned man; He marched to Calvary as the conscious Master of His own death. His life was not taken, but given in all the freedom of deliberate choice. In His agony He became more than conqueror, uttering words of compassion, "Father, forgive them; for they know not what they do" (Luke 23:34). We can then understand why even a tough centurion, hardened to the sight of men dying in shame, would in a flash of revelation exclaim: "I never saw anyone die like Jesus. Truly, He must be the Son of God" (see Mark 15:39).

B. *A Sacrifice*

In the cross of Jesus is also a sacrifice. The prophet said of Jesus: "Who did no sin, neither was guile found in his mouth" (1 Pet. 2:22, quoting Isa. 53:9). Jesus had no business from a moral standpoint being there. Why then did He die? There is only one answer, and Paul gives it in language that even a child can grasp: "Christ died as a sacrifice for us in our sins" (see Rom. 5:8).

Let us get a picture of the blackness of sin as we stand before the wondrous Cross. Let's not speak only of external behavior, but of inner pride and self-sufficiency, of our arrogant usurping of the place of God and the vicious cycle of our own egotism.

When we begin to contemplate both outwardly and inwardly, we see what Christ really had to die for. We see ourselves as we really are with all pretensions, excuses, and illusions torn away. No longer can we rationalize and

139

explain ourselves. I not only see the treachery of Judas, the scheming of Caiaphas, the compromise of Pilate, the disloyalty of Peter, but I see in myself those things which necessitated the sacrifice of God's Son.

I see in the Cross the immense cost of my salvation. Christ died for my sins. Where my sin abounded, grace did much more abound. Jesus took my place and He paid the price which I cannot pay. It cost His blood and Peter reminds with a bold affirmation, "You know that you were ransomed . . . not with perishable things such as silver or gold, but the precious blood of Christ" (1 Pet. 1:18-19, RSV). When I look at the Cross, I can only say, "God gave himself for me; He forgives me at His sacrifice."

C. A Call to Commitment

I also see in the Cross a call to commitment. The death of Jesus not only means that something amazing was done for me, but that something demanding is expected of me. "Love so amazing, so divine, Demands my soul, my life, my all."

The cross of Christ is a demand. No less than a total sacrifice of myself to Jesus will do. No other than giving the will of Christ priority over my most cherished interests and ambitions will suffice.

"To this you have been called," said Peter, "because Christ also suffered for you, leaving you an example, that you should follow in his steps" (1 Pet. 2:21, RSV). For the Christians who take the Cross seriously, there is no such thing as part-time surrender. It is truly a call to commitment.

III. Conclusion

At the Passion Play at Oberammergau this year, a reporter went backstage to meet the man who played the part of Christ. Noticing the great cross which was carried, he stooped down to lift it to his shoulder, but he couldn't move it more than an inch off the floor. It was made of heavy oak beams. Amazed, the reporter turned to the actor and said, "I thought it would be light and hollow. Why must you carry a cross so heavy?" The actor replied softly, "Sir, if I did not feel the weight of His cross, I could not play His part."

We must feel the weight and the power of the Cross if we are to truly play a part in the world's redemption. The one who has really experienced the Cross will finally cry with the songwriter: "Were the whole realm of nature mine, / That were an offering far too small. / Love so amazing, so divine, / *shall have* my soul, my life, my all" (italicized words inserted).

Come to the table; see the Cross in its dimensions of victory, sacrifice, and challenge. Draw freely from the forgiving, empowering love of Christ as He ministers to you through the remembrance of His shed blood. You will not be the same.

Where to Find God

SCRIPTURE: 2 Kings 5:1-4

I. Introduction

One of the great devotional writers of our age says that there is a great difference in looking for God and finding Him. Many people look for God but they never find Him, for they look in the wrong places.

It was that quotation which led me to a story very deep within the Second Book of Kings—the story of the Assyrian general called Naaman and the Israelite prophet, Elisha. It is a story of a man who went looking for God and how God found him instead.

Naaman, we are told, was a commander of the army of the king of Syria, a great man with his master, in high favor of mighty men of valor—"*but* he was a leper" (v. 1). Naaman is not too much different from us, is he? We are perhaps not great, but we are good and in favor, respected by those who know us. We are people with valor; that is, with determination to do the right thing, but something is missing. Something is wrong—"but he was a leper." We want something more than just being good. We are looking for that which will really put life together and heal some of the inner distress that we feel in our lack of fulfillment.

Let's probe the story of Naaman to see if it has anything to say to us. The circumstances and the roles are different, but perhaps the spiritual lesson will apply to us as well.

II. The Context

A. *Method*

The answer for Naaman was a little captive servant girl who suggested to Naaman's wife, who in turn suggested to her husband that there was a prophet in Israel who could cure leprosy. Let's not dismiss the little people in life, for through their obedience great things have happened. If you are one, take note that God can use your openness to Him, just as He used the servant girl's obedience.

B. *Approach*

How was Naaman going to cure his leprosy? Of course, in a manner worthy of Naaman. So he proceeded to find God by going through kings and protocol. Then loaded with protocol and gifts, he figured that a king's audience and some $80,000 worth of gifts would be enough to impress this Hebrew prophet and his God.

Sounds ridiculous, doesn't it? But does it? Do we not often look for God in ways that befit God's stature—and ours too? Are we tempted to think that our approach to God must be impressive, especially if we are a bit impressed with ourselves? The common, ordinary things of life, it is easy to believe, are too low for God to be present. So we look for Him in the impressive, the dazzling—thoughtfully prepared.

C. *Problem*

We shouldn't be too surprised by Naaman's reaction when Elisha did not come out and pray before him and wave his hand over the place and cure his leprosy. Naaman was clearly irked. After all this impressive preparation to find God, all he found was a common prophet living in a low-income housing development, not at all concerned about putting on an impressive show to cure Naaman.

The result of Naaman's reaction? He almost lost God a couple times. First, his approach through the king backfired when the king of Israel suspected that Naaman was up to some international spying. Then Naaman lost his temper because Elisha wasn't impressed by him, his horses, chariots, and fabulous gifts. Elisha, in fact, didn't even come out of the house to greet him, but sent out his servant telling Naaman simply to wash seven times in the revoltingly filthy waters of the river Jordan. At that point, Naaman was about ready to give up and hang it all and go home.

D. *Answer*

But God didn't get lost for Naaman because God began to become the Searcher for Naaman. While Naaman was absorbed in kings and protocol, God was beginning to work as He often works—through the most common and unlikely people, things, and methods. First, we have already mentioned that He worked through that captive servant girl. Then God began to work through Naaman's

143

common old servants—the ones who calmed him down after he flew into a rage, who said to him: "Look, if Elisha asked you to do some great thing, would you not have done it? Then try the easy thing and wash in a river."

Naaman relented and went to the river, dipped himself in and out seven times, and found that for all his looking, God had actually found him through the common and unlikely lips and methods.

III. Lesson

A. *The Potential Importance of the "Unimportant"*

This story has much to say about God's way with us. One is the potential importance of the unimportant. While we are often preoccupied with that which is impressive, God works often in His own way through the most unlikely events and people. God speaks to you often where you least expect to hear His voice—through the unlikely lips of your children, or the common but mature saint of God. God speaks to us through some of the common events of life, perhaps through the thankfulness of a friend with a desperate need, sharing of your meal with a lonely visitor at church, through the rather broken testimony of someone at prayer meeting, or the leaping out of a familiar passage of the Bible in new truth.

Don't overlook the common. It comprises 90 percent of life. God speaks through it far more than through the impressive.

B. *The Power of a Small Event*

God would like to speak to us through some of the most common materials of our existence—bread and juice. We tend to think of the sacrament of the Lord's Supper as something very extraordinary or superhuman. In one sense it is. Like all meaningful symbols, the bread and juice contain some of the power of the thing which they symbolize. A piece of colored cloth, a flag for instance, has the power to move men to the same kind of fervor and action that the nation itself can. Or if we hear somebody's name (a symbol for the person himself), sometimes it has the power to make our hearts beat fast or strike fear into our souls.

It is so with the elements of the Lord's Supper before us. If we let them, they will communicate the power of Jesus Christ. Not just the power to make the heart beat faster, but the power to bring forgiveness, healing, transformation to our life, to help us find a new dimension of life, to find healing, like Naaman.

IV. Conclusion

There is a considerable difference between looking for God and finding Him. You and I are tempted to think sometimes that God is to be found through the impressive. God, however, is generally in the most common things of life, like the elements gathered before us and prepared for our use. All God asks is that, like Naaman, we come to ourselves and accept ourselves for what we are in the eyes of God. All He asks is that you come to Him without pretension, simply as a person in need of something, and He will give it to you.

I ask you to come to the Lord's table this morning and partake of the elements. Whatever your need is—rededication, forgiveness, restoration of relationships, solutions, guidance, whatever it be—let the presence of God in these common elements find you and lead you and restore you to spiritual health.

Songs of Restoration

SCRIPTURE: Psalm 107, RSV

I. Introduction

If we would put in one phrase the message of this psalm, it would have to be: "God's love never gives up." The Psalmist shows us that what finally gets to us and breaks the back of our rebellion and sets us free from our emotional hang-ups is the unqualified love of God which never lets us go. He accepts us as we are and then sets about to make us what we ourselves are longing to be. That activity of God is what the Psalmist calls "the steadfast love of God."

The psalm is very simple in its structure. It is divided into two major parts after the opening sentence which introduces it.

II. The Works of God

Here we have four testimonies of people who experienced the work of God in the midst of crisis. Let's review them.

A. *The Restless* (vv. 4-9)

"Some wandered in desert wastes, finding no way to a city to dwell in; hungry and thirsty, their soul fainted within them." Who are these? They are what we might call the restless ones. They are the ones that wander about from place to place, or job to job, or marriage to marriage, filled with questions and seeking to find where the answer lies. There are a lot of them today.

Certainly there is nothing wrong with excitement. Excitement is a quality we need in life. Life was also intended to be secure—to give us a place where we feel at home, at rest, relaxed. That is what these people are looking for, but they cannot find it. They are "hungry and thirsty," the Psalmist says, which means that their cravings have not been satisfied.

Then we are told how they find satisfaction. "Then they cried to the Lord in their trouble, and he delivered them from their distress; he led them by a straight way, till they reached a city to dwell in." Some of you have had this experience. You, too, were restless, uncertain, wandering. You were hungry and thirsty for life, but you could never find it. You tried everything; finally when you reached the bottom, you cried to the Lord in your trouble. When you did, He heard you. Not suddenly or instantaneously, but gradually He began to set you free. He began to lead you by a straight way. That is the way described in the scripture—a straight way, right through the middle of life. God leads them until they reach the place of excitement and security. But it does not happen overnight; sometimes it takes a while.

B. *Bound-up* (vv. 10-16)

Now here is another testimony: "Some sat in darkness and in gloom, prisoners in affliction and in irons, for they had rebelled against the words of God, and spurned the counsel of the Most High. Their hearts were bowed down with hard labor; they fell down, with none to help." Who are these? These we might call the bound-up ones.

Notice their conditions: They sit in darkness and gloom. That is always the figure in the Bible for confusion. Their lives are filled with gloom; they have no hope, but they do not know what is wrong. More than that, they are "in irons." They are a prisoner of certain habits, ideas, thoughts, attitudes that hold them in an iron grip.

The Psalmist indicates the cause: "It is because they rebelled against the words of God." In other words, they did not like what God said about life, and they chose to act on what they felt, not realizing that God was telling them the truth. Second, they "spurned the counsel of the Most High." That is, since they did not like what God said, they decided not to follow what He commanded. They turned aside from it and thus they found themselves "bowed down with hard labor." Do you know what inevitably follows? The person who is trying to do it all by himself is already in trouble.

But God does not leave them there. That is the beauty of this. No, listen: "Then they cried to the Lord in their trouble, and he delivered them from their distress." It tells us what He did. "He brought them out of darkness and gloom." That was the first step. He opened their eyes to show them that what they were rebelling against was reality. His words are a revelation of the way things are.

When this one cried to God, he found a power to act which he never had before. He rose up with a new kind of power, suddenly, just like that.

This does not mean that they did not have a struggle. The struggle was on different terms from then on. It was no longer a struggle to break free, but to keep from sliding back again.

C. *The Neurotics* (vv. 17-22)

Now the next condition: "Some were sick through their sinful ways, and because of their iniquities suffered affliction; they loathed any kind of food, and they drew near to the gates of death." Here are the neurotics. They are sick people who are physically or emotionally sick. Aren't these interesting characteristics. First, they loathe healthy food. Now food is what the body requires and, figuratively, is what the soul requires. These neurotic people are charac-

148

terized by the fact that they do not want healthy things. They do not want good food. They don't want to read good books, they want highly spiced literature that sets them tingling and panders to their desires. This is all they want to live on. Therefore, they get worse. Here are sick people—neurotic people, unable to handle life. They are fearful, nervous, and afraid to go out and face life as it is.

Then what happened? "Then they cried to the Lord in their trouble, and he delivered them from their distress; he sent forth his word, and healed them, and delivered them from destruction."

When the Psalmist says, "He sent his word," it does not mean that God gave them a Bible to read. It means that He identified with them. The Lord Jesus is called the Word of God, the Living Word, the Logos, the Word that became flesh and dwelt among us. Thus, when it says that God sent His word and healed them, it means that some way He moved in right where they were. He identified with them, He did not reject these neurotics because they were difficult to live with.

Jesus said: "If you continue in my word . . . you will know the truth, and the truth will make you free" (John 8:31-32, RSV). Isn't that tremendous? How many have been set free as they have begun to understand the truth about themselves and life through the Word.

D. *The Devastated* (vv. 23-32)

Let's look at the next type of people: "Some went down to the sea in ships, doing business on the great waters; they saw the deeds of the Lord, his wondrous works in the deep. For he commanded, and raised the stormy wind, which lifted up the waves of the sea. They mounted up to heaven, they went down to the depths; their courage melted away in their evil plight; they reeled and

149

staggered like drunken men, and were at their wits' end."
Here we have the devastated ones.

We know devastation too, don't we? What can we learn
from this? Here is the account of people who are engaged
in the normal practices of life when a crisis arises. They
have been counting on themselves, thinking they had what
it takes to handle their affairs. Suddenly a crisis of overwhelming proportion arises, and they do not know what to
do or where to turn. But at last they turned to the Lord and
discovered that He, and He alone, is capable of getting them
to their desired haven.

Here are the works of God. In this psalm he delivers
the restless, the neurotic, the bound-up, and the devastated—those who are sick or are wandering and are un-
satisfied. He delivers them by that unconditional love which
keeps after them and will never let them go. This is what
sets them free.

III. The Way of God

The latter part of the psalm describes the way God does
this, His methodology.

A. *He Supplies.* (vv. 33-38)

"He turns rivers into a desert, springs of water into
thirsty ground, a fruitful land into a salty waste, because of
the wickedness of its inhabitants."

First, to accomplish His purposes God uses adversity.
He deliberately, at times, sends into our pathway trouble
and disaster because it is the only way He can get our
attention.

C. S. Lewis put it this way: "God whispers to us in our
pleasures, speaks to us in our consciences, but shouts at us
in our pain."

Second, God can also use prosperity. "He turns a desert

into pools of water, a parched land into springs of water. And there he lets the hungry dwell, and they establish a city to live in; they sow fields, and plant vineyards, and get a fruitful yield. By His blessing they multiply greatly; and he does not let their cattle decrease." When you take God at His word, you walk in the fullness of His strength and supply. You begin to fellowship with Him and enjoy His presence. Sometimes He rewards you. He sends the very thing you are looking for. He meets your needs, satisfies your heart, and fills you with good things. Your prayers do not go unanswered, for God moves to meet your needs and protects you.

B. *He Protects.* (vv. 39-41)

"When they are diminished and brought low through oppression, trouble, and sorrow, he pours contempt upon princes [they are your enemies] and makes them wander in trackless wastes; but he raises up the needy out of affliction, and makes their families like flocks."

C. *He Vindicates.* (v. 42)

Finally, at the end of the psalm we get the reaction of people to this: "The upright see it and are glad." That is, if you are beginning to understand God and relate to Him, you can see these two things and neither one disturbs you. If things get rough, it does not bother you. "For I have learned, in whatever state I am, to be content. Whether I am abased or abound, it does not make any difference, because God knows what He is doing" (see Phil. 4:11-12).

The wicked have nothing left to say. That is what God says will happen to the upright man. As he works his way through life and men become aware of the whole story of how God acts, they simply have nothing to say; they are reduced to silence. It becomes evident that God is fair and just in what He does, and no person can complain.

IV. Conclusion

So the last word is one of admonition. "Whoever is wise, let him give heed to these things; let men consider the steadfast love of the Lord" (v. 43). That means, think about all this. There are people here who have been going through one or more of these difficult situations. Some are wandering, restless, hostile, or bitter. They are held prisoner by some attitude, outlook, or habit. Or they are sick, neurotic, emotionally upset. Perhaps some are fearful, troubled by a crisis into which they have come. Alright, stop and think about how God accepts you, how He loves you, how He is deeply concerned about you and will meet you right where you are and take you just as you are. His love does not change a bit. He is concerned about you and has already received you, already given you all that He can give in Christ Jesus. Alright, then—begin to rejoice in that fact. You will find that love will set you free so that you can act upon the power and liberty that God gives.

Let's allow our experience of the sacraments of Communion to restore us to the place we desire.

What's This Thing Called Grace?

SCRIPTURE: John 8:1-11, RSV

I. Introduction

By way of introduction of partaking in the sacrament of Communion, I want to call attention to one of the encounters of Jesus out of which comes some tremendous insights. It centers around the woman who had been caught in adultery. Placing her in the midst of the circle around Jesus, the scribes and Pharisees challenge Him: " 'Teacher, this woman has been caught in the act of adultery. Now in the law Moses commanded us to stone such. What do you say about her?' This they said to test him, that they might have some charge to bring against him."

If you have been in a "no-win" situation, you can identify with where Jesus seems to be at this moment. We can almost see the whirling in the scribes' and Pharisees' minds. In their judgment, Jesus cannot win in any way in this encounter.

But even beyond the dilemma is a further complication in this situation, and that is that Jesus faces two kinds of sin. The one is obvious: the sin of the woman. The other is the sin of the scribes. It is the sin of selfish insensitivity. What is He going to do in this situation? How can He win? On the one hand He has to support who He is (the fulfillment of the law) and keep that in focus. On the other hand, He has the whole spiritual, moral dilemma in the participants of this drama. What is Jesus going to do in such a situation?

Jesus' response is to confront them. He stands and charges them: "Let him who is without sin among you be the first to throw a stone at her." He bends down and writes with his finger on the ground; and when they hear it, they go away one by one. He shifts the trial, the test completely and comes back to them. They were asking Him if He was the Messiah, and He asked them if *they* were the Messiah. It was as if Jesus is responding, "Let's answer the question in parts. He wants to know if I am the Messiah. Before we decide whether I am, let's decide whether there are any other possible Messiahs out here. Anyone who is a Messiah throw the first rock." When they are all gone, the woman is left standing by herself. Jesus looks up and asks her, "Woman, where are they? Has no one condemned you?" She replies, "No one, Lord." Jesus assures her, "Neither do I condemn you; go, and do not sin again."

II. The Marks of Grace

Let's interpret the significance of this incredible event. What happens here is that the two great marks of our Lord's grace are brought together.

A. *Sovereignty*

The first mark is that of His Lordship, His sovereignty. What we see in this passage is an example of the Lordship of Jesus. Every single person standing in that crowd is being encountered authoritatively by Jesus. They come as a mob, but by the time it is finished, every single one of them is facing a question: "Am I without sin enough to throw my stone?" Here our Lord is showing His strength. The incidents in this narrative are revealing, like the brooding silence and mystery of His handwriting in the sand.

This is the Lordship of Jesus Christ. This is what it means for these men to be judged by our Lord. They ask Him to play the role of judge, and He does. In effect, He turns their pride into guilt, and He strips them of their idols.

One of the primary manifestations of the grace of Christ is to strip us of our idols. The first thing His grace does is to take away every idol we have, to remove our claims to be autonomous, to scatter our proud imaginations. These men go to see a judge, and what a judge they get!

But the woman is also judged. This may sound surprising; we may think she is only forgiven, but she is also judged by our Lord. I believe that the presence of those men, in a sense, make the woman feel less guilty than she should. She is no fool. She knows the guilty male partner is set free. As they bring her, she knows she is being used as an object

154

lesson. She knows that the people bringing her to Jesus are hypocrites. They are no better than she is. Though she may feel guilty for having been caught in the act of adultery, that guilt is overwhelmed by her sense of rationalization and bitterness towards those men for what they are doing.

Now, when not a soul is standing around except this woman after Jesus has judged them, He looks to this lone person: "Woman, where are your accusers?" She looks up, and when she cannot see anyone standing there, answers: "They have all gone." I think it is now that her guilt is the greatest, as she knows that her accusers are nonexistent. There is no one to feel angry at except herself. She is now fully in view of her own self and her own problem. Jesus has scattered all the superficial judges so that now she is left standing only before Him. The sovereignty of His judgment is more profound when I cannot lay it on someone else.

Lordship and judgment are a part of the grace of God. It's His move to scatter our idols and view ourselves as we really are—sinners in need of forgiveness.

B. *Acceptance*

Now we are ready to see the second and greatest mark of the grace of our Lord. Now we are shown the grace of Jesus Christ in the act of forgiveness of the woman. What an incredible moment that is. The crowd is far away; the woman is fully aware of her own responsibility. Jesus asks, "Woman, has no one condemned you?" She responds, "No one, Lord." He affirms, "Neither do I. Go and sin no more."

In that event, the Lord set this very concrete person, just like many people, free; free from the *present* (symbolized by her accusers); free from the *past* (the fact of her experience); and free *for* the future (challenged to be something better).

But notice when He does that. He absorbs within himself her sin, for He got himself into trouble by setting this woman free. He has taken her guilt, her problem, the responsibility for it upon himself. It is now all on His shoulders—and *that* is the meaning of the Cross.

III. Conclusion

The Cross is where Jesus Christ died by His own free choice to take upon His shoulders the sin of that crowd, the sin of this woman, our own sin and confusion. He bears it, He disarms it.

Some Bible versions, rather than placing this passage in the regular place, have put it in the footnotes of the 8th chapter of John. In other manuscripts it appears in another place, such as the 21st chapter of Luke, after the 38th verse. If it is true that this event occurred in the sequence of Luke 21, then this would be the last person Jesus encountered before the Last Supper, because this passage would be just before Judas betrays Him into the hands of His captors. In any case, this event may have triggered the death coalition against Jesus. What more charges do the scribes need? For Jesus took on His shoulder the sin of that whole episode. Whether in John or Luke, the Lord stirred the furious opposition of His enemies.

What is this thing called grace? It is Jesus Christ taking upon His shoulders the responsibility of our sins, our confusions. It is Jesus bearing it for us and thus setting us free to follow Him.

The same Lord stands before us today. Where do you stand with Him? Is it the sin of pride haunting you? Are you still erecting all kinds of tests and roadblocks for Christ, stripping Him of His Messiahship, trying to take it upon yourself? Are you like the woman, trapped, embittered, unable to defend yourself, rationalizing—how do you feel? Is it the sin of arrogance, rocks clutched in your hands; or the sin of being completely undone, but refusing to accept responsibility for it?

Hear the gospel of Christ. Our Lord has broken through to release you from every captivity so that every one of us may stand before Him to hear these words: "Who judges you?" We look around to our amazement and find that there is no judge now except Christ in the room. "Neither do I judge you; go and sin no more. Follow Me and be My disciple." I invite you to meet the Lord and to do it through taking His body and His blood by faith, as symbolized through these elements into your life.

BILL M. SULLIVAN is director of the Division of Church Growth of the Church of the Nazarene. A native of Arkansas, he graduated from Bethany Nazarene College (1954) and Nazarene Theological Seminary (1957). His ministerial career has included being pastor of Denver Westminster Church, director of public relations of Bethany Nazarene College, and pastor of Colorado Springs First Church. On the Colorado District he was District Church Schools chairman, member of the District Advisory Board, and a member of the Board of Regents of Northwest Nazarene College.

In 1975 he became superintendent of the North Carolina District and served in that leadership position until he was named to the post he now fills in 1980.

THANKSGIVING

Bill M. Sullivan

The observance of special days is one way the church can be relevant in the lives of people. At the major holiday seasons, people in general are thinking about the particular emphasis. Frequently they are celebrating the event in some manner. When the church programs for and speaks to the event being celebrated, its message is reinforced by other aspects of the special occasion. The church also identifies with society at a point of common interest.

Thanksgiving Day is a special occasion that offers particular opportunity to the church. Because the observance is rooted in our national heritage, it has a particular appeal to citizens. Because the thanksgiving has always been understood as directed toward God, the observance is very much at home in the church. Also, because thanksgiving is a dominant theme of the Bible, there is a wide range of topics to emphasize in sermons, songs, and celebrations.

Because Thanksgiving Day deals with our national heritage, it has accumulated its share of sentimentalism. It rather easily displays a distorted backdrop from which a folk theology of God is derived. For this reason it is important for the minister to speak clearly to the issues involved. As a pastor, my approach was to face squarely the realities of life in this world. Every time I stood up to preach a Thanksgiving sermon, I knew I was looking into the faces of some people who were at their wits end. Life had not been kind to them, and I could not ignore that fact as I called on the congregation to express special thanks to God.

I was usually able to satisfy my heart and mind by building a rational base for gratitude to God. Of course the rational base assumed faith in the Word of God. While I wasn't able to unravel the mystery of evil and human suffering, it was possible to bring some reasoned understanding to the subject.

From this point I proceeded to emphasize the many reasons for and values of gratefulness in people's lives. The discourse followed whatever facet of the truth that happened to appeal to me each year. I liked to give each year a freshness rather than letting it become a tired repetition. Of course I had to guard against missing the point for the sake of uniqueness. However, there are more ways to approach a sermon on thanksgiving than at first appears.

Thanksgiving really grows out of an attitude of gratitude. It is important that people not only say thanks but that they feel thankful. This, of course, depends upon their recognition of the Source of their material benefits. Gratefulness is more than a matter of knowledge. It must be a spirit that is constantly cultivated. Part of the cultivation process is the public worship and praise of God. While praise is a part of every service, Thanksgiving provides an opportunity for extraordinary expressions of praise.

I wanted Thanksgiving Sunday to be such a grand celebration of the goodness of God to the children of men that people would be motivated by it for an extended period. Thus, we focused on the greatness and kindness of God to all mankind. We sought to glorify, praise, honor, and thank Him. This happy experience of corporate praise was intended to reinforce the idea that gratitude brings joy to life all year long.

God's Open Hand

SCRIPTURE: Ps. 145:13*b*-21

TEXT: *You open your hand and satisfy the desires of every living thing* (v. 16, NIV).

It was reported that in South Africa, March 16, 1963, a Capetown University medical student, John Keough, claimed the world's handshaking record with sixty thousand shakes in an hour. I don't see how that was possible. The rate of 60,000 an hour would be 1,000 per minute or more than 16 handshakes a second. He may have touched 60,000 people in one hour, but I doubt that he shook their hands.

A British poet playfully claims that he is a bona fide poet because he is only five handshakes away from Shelley. He declares that he once shook hands with the poet Swinburne, who once shook hands with the poet Southey, who in turn shook hands with Walter Savage Landor, who was an intimate friend of Shelley. So he figures he is only five handshakes away from Shelley.

I suppose that I am not more than five handshakes away from John Wesley. I think I recall shaking hands with Bishop Gerald Kennedy. When he was ordained, he must have shaken hands with the bishop who was surely much older than he. That's only two handshakes removed from Bishop Matthew Simpson, who shook hands with Bishop William McKendree. McKendree was ordained by Francis Asbury, who was sent to America by John Wesley. We can be sure that Wesley shook hands with Asbury when he said good-by. That means I am only five handshakes away from Wesley.

This is a game which we all can play. Some of you may be only one or two handshakes away from Lincoln or other great American personalities.

Yet, even though you may be only one handshake removed from a great person, that's a long way. It could mean that you've never even seen the person!

The truth is that we may actually shake hands with great people today and yet be removed by a vast chasm of unconcern. It's very easy to be physically close to people yet actually so far away.

We live in a world of increasing anonymity. We live our own lives and just let the rest of the world go by. Consequently, not only are our lives closed to others, but their lives are closed to us.

Modern man, in the midst of a megalopolis, is alone. Everywhere he turns, lives are closed to him. Instead of the open hand of community and civic camaraderie, all he can see is the clenched fist of resentment and retaliation.

There are many *concealed* hands. They are instruments of deception. The hand is quicker than the eye. How easily we are victimized by the crafty hand.

But percentage wise the clenched fist and concealed hand are in the minority. For the most part we can avoid them. It's the *unextended* hand that really hurts us. You know how it feels to be slighted by a person with whom you want to shake hands. It is not only embarrassing—it hurts. To seek an open hand and find it closed is a wounding disappointment.

So many hands are closed to us. But God's hand is open! We have a God whose hands are open. Think what that means. Though all the other hands in the world are closed, His hands are open.

His open hands *welcome* us. He always has time for us and is interested in us. He receives the sinner with outstretched arms and open hands. He invites, "Come to me, all you who are weary and burdened, and I will give you rest" (Matt. 11:28, NIV).

The parable of the prodigal son is the story of a sinful boy who returns to the open hands and outstretched arms of a waiting father. It is a picture of God.

God's hands are open to His children. We are told to approach His throne with confidence "so that we may receive mercy and find grace to help us in our time of need" (Heb. 4:16, NIV).

His hands *lift* us. Said the Psalmist, "He lifted me out of the slimy pit, out of the mud and mire; he set my feet on a rock" (Ps. 40:2, NIV). God has sent us a message through Isaiah the prophet. "Do not fear, for I am with you; do not be dismayed, for I am your God. I will strengthen you and help you; I will uphold you with my righteous right hand" (Isa. 41:10, NIV).

Yes, His hands are open to *save*, to *help*, to *lift*, to *give*. In our text, the Psalmist observes, "Thou openest thy hand, thou satisfiest the desire of every living thing" (RSV).

What's in the hand of God? Certainly every material need of our lives is in His benevolent hand. He is the God of harvest and in His hand are abundant provisions. He satisfies the desire of every living creature.

But at this Thanksgiving time, it is important to realize that more than material blessings come from God.

The Psalmist declares, "My times are in your hands" (Ps. 31:15, NIV). With him we all must agree. Both the longevity and destiny of our lives are in His hand. If we believe in a God who is interested in the details of our lives, we must admit that we live only by the permission of His will. We can be thankful that our destiny is His perpetual concern. The Holy Spirit is interceding for us at God's throne continually (Rom. 8:26).

Jesus assures us that His followers are in the Father's hand, and "no one can snatch them out of my Father's

163

hand" (John 10:29, NIV). I don't believe in what is commonly called eternal security, but I praise God for the security of believers.

Some of us grew up with the idea that God was a spiritual policeman who was anxious to punish us for every deviation. The truth is that He is doing everything in His power to keep us in His fellowship. He will not tolerate willful sin, but whoever puts his faith in Him will have the protection of heaven over his soul. The poet expressed this truth in declaring,

> The soul that on Jesus hath leaned for repose
> I will not, I will not desert to his foes;
> That soul, though all hell should endeavor to shake,
> I'll never, no never, no never forsake.

I like to believe that the ministers of God are in His hand. When John saw a vision of the Lord on the isle of Patmos, he described that "in his right hand he held seven stars" (Rev. 1:16, NIV). These were angels or messengers to the particular churches. If they were angels, I lose my case. But if they were messengers, I'd like to identify with them.

In this same vision, John told of Christ laying His right hand upon him, declaring, "I hold the keys of death and Hades" (v. 18, NIV). Christ died and now is alive forevermore. And because He lives, we shall live also. If only one possession was left in the hand of God, let it be the key to the back door of death. I want out of there, and Christ is the only One I know who has the key. He opens His hand and satisfies the desire of every living creature. My desire is for eternal life. Thank God, the key is in His hand.

We could extend the list of things that are in God's hand. But John's Gospel declares that He "has placed everything in his [Jesus'] hands" (John 3:35; cf. 13:3, NIV). No wonder when He opens His hand, He satisfies the desire of every living thing.

Why Is Thanksgiving So Important?

TEXT: *In every thing give thanks: for this is the will of God in Christ Jesus concerning you* (1 Thess. 5:18; cf. Eph. 5:20; Phil. 4:6; Col. 3:17).

Unless we are thankful, we're not emotionally healthy. Or, to put it another way, we're out of touch with reality. For all of us owe so much of what we are and enjoy to other people, people to whom we owe thanks—and to whom we should occasionally express it.

But, of course, a lack of gratitude is far more serious than depriving a worthy person of some much-deserved expressions of appreciation. Unthankfulness represents either self-obsession or resentment of others. Neither condition is emotionally healthy.

The person who is engrossed in himself is badly disoriented to life. He will not find happiness because people will not like him. Life will be cruel to him, at least as seen through his own eyes.

Likewise, the person who resents others has shut himself off from his only means of meaningful joy. And he has reached some false conclusions which will make his life a chain reaction of errors.

All this is true quite apart from Christianity and spirituality. There are many people who are not really religious and yet recognize their debt to others. They are grateful to parents, friends, teachers, and associates. They may be lacking in spiritual understanding and commitment, but they are, at least, aware of their physical interdependence or even origin, for that matter. Of course, it is true that God made us, but there's even more for which to be grateful than that.

Our text exhorts us to "give thanks in all circumstances" (NIV). This links gratitude not merely to the past, but also to present and potential conditions.

All of the verses express a sort of reckless thankfulness for not just some of the good things, but for everything.

At first this sounds like a simple overstatement of the case. Hasty generalizations under the impulse of the moment are understandable. Surely, if the apostle Paul had stopped to think about it, he would have qualified his remarks. Perhaps he would have added, "Well, at least give thanks for those things that you believe are God's will for you."

But that's not what he said, and the evidence is rather clear that he had no intention of involving any such thing. In four different letters to four different churches, he declared essentially the same truth—"give thanks in *all* circumstances!"

What's more, he even added, "For this is God's will for you in Christ Jesus" (1 Thess. 5:18, NIV).

To give thanks in all circumstances is God's will? Why would the apostle Paul want to make a point of that? Indeed why would it be God's will for us to express gratitude for all of life's circumstances? Why is thankfulness so important?

I. To Be Thankful in Every Circumstance Forces Us to Believe in a Divine Plan.

We are confident "that in all things God works for the good of those who love him, who have been called according to his purpose" (Rom. 8:28, NIV). We do not know why we are beset with evil and suffering. The Bible teaches that God can take any circumstance and convert it into an avenue of blessing.

166

Let's be specific. Do you think God is going to take that bitter disappointment in your life and make it a stepping-stone to greater joy and fulfillment? Do you believe God can fit it into a plan for good in your life? Unless you believe that, there's no way you can be thankful for your present circumstances.

I don't know of any way you can escape from your predicament. I'm quite sure you'll cry again. Yes, you'll feel lonely and blue. But there's still a good word for you. God knows how and is planning right now to convert that overwhelming experience into a stepping-stone of life.

Yes, to be thankful in all circumstances does force us to believe in a divine plan.

II. It Is Also the Only Way We Can Retain Peace and Joy in Our Christian Experience.

When we lose our sense of gratitude, we have also lost our peace and joy. Life is a variety of experiences. Unless we see them all as occasions for thankfulness, we will constantly be thrashing around, trying to escape misfortune and distress.

God wants us to be at peace about what is happening in our lives. I know it sounds like a contradiction—even an impossibility. But all the evidence points to the truth of this assertion.

Recall what Jesus said to His disciples: "I'm going to be crucified," He revealed (cf. Matt. 26:2, NIV). "I'm going away," He told them (John 14:28, NIV). "All men will hate you because of me" (Mark 13:13, NIV), He explained. He even assured them they would be killed by religious zealots. Yet, to this bewildered group, staggering under the rapid blows of such prophecy, He declared, "Peace I leave with you; my peace I give you" (John 14:27, NIV).

It seems incredible that He would say that to His disciples, and even more so that they would believe it. But that's just the way it happened. And it can happen that way to us. In the midst of our sorrow we can have the peace of God that passes all understanding.

But we can't have the peace without the faith that makes it possible for us to thank God for all the circumstances of our lives.

III. Observe Now that to Be Thankful in All Circumstances Is the Only Attitude Consistent with Witness and Compatible with Worship.

Thankfulness is important because of the faith it demonstrates. How can we convince the world of God's existence and goodness if we are exhibiting displeasure with what He has allowed our lot in life to be?

It is a powerful witness whenever a Christian is able to face adversity not merely bravely but with gratitude for God's control of all things.

Gratitude is also the only attitude compatible with worship. Unless we can find it in our hearts to thank God for the life He has given us, we will not be able to praise and worship Him.

This is really the crucible for many people. When they become unhappy with their lot in life, they become dissatisfied with God and His operation in the world as well as in their lives. They lose their ability to worship and praise God, which only means that their whole relationship with God is in trouble.

It is important for us to always maintain our gratitude to God. Regardless of circumstances, God is still in control.

Thanksgiving is an especially good time to remind ourselves of all the blessings we receive from His beneficent hand. But particularly this year let us remember that even those things which seem unfortunate are nonetheless occasions for gratitude.

Therefore, with faith and joy we wholeheartedly demonstrate this day our concurrence with Paul's exhortation to "give thanks in all circumstances, for this is God's will for you in Christ Jesus" (NIV).

Gratitude for the Things
That Make a Life

Scripture: Luke 12:13-21

Sometimes it seems like Jesus is too otherworldly. This God-man who lived in our kind of world for 33 years surely must have understood the human predicament. The Bible declares that He was subjected to all the temptations that a human being can experience. The Old Testament prophet, Isaiah, foresaw that Jesus would be "a man of sorrows, and acquainted with grief." In the early centuries the Church had to come to terms with the kind of man Jesus was. Was He really God or just a divinely anointed man? Was He really man or just the appearance of a man? In the crucible of one of the greatest struggles the Church has ever known, it declared unequivocally that Jesus Christ was not only fully God, but also fully man!

With the very plain statement of the Bible and the carefully thought-out position of the Church we have every reason to believe that Jesus Christ understood to the fullest extent what it meant to be a human being.

But why was He then, on occasion, so otherworldly? Why did He place so much emphasis on spiritual things and give such little place to material things?

In the Sermon on the Mount Jesus instructed His followers, "Do not worry about your life, what you will eat; or about your body, what you will wear. Life is more than food, and the body more than clothes" (Luke 12:22-23, NIV).

We all know material things are important, and to some degree essential. In defense of Jesus' teaching we must point out that He never says material things are unimportant, although we sometimes infer that from His teaching.

What He does say is that in comparison to spiritual realities, material things are of considerably less value. One materialist declared that money isn't everything, but it sure beats whatever is in second place! Jesus, who was spiritually oriented, would have come back with, "Spiritual realities aren't everything there is to life, but they are a million miles ahead of material things!"

Our problem today isn't simply our interest in material things, but our lack of appreciation for spiritual realities. That's the way we should look at this scripture. If a man's life doesn't consist in an abundance of possessions, then in what does it consist? And when we discover the real essence of life, let us, during this Thanksgiving season, be grateful for the things that make a life.

New concepts in psychiatry postulate man's mental health to center in the fulfillment of two basic human needs, the need to both love and to be loved and the need to feel worthwhile to ourself and to others.

Let's look at these needs in Christian terms.

I. We Can Say that, as Christians, the Things That Make Our Lives Are People and Possibilities.

People are an essential ingredient of life. None of us can exist without them. We must have people to love us and to whom we can express our love in return. Our lives not

170

only are, but must be, intertwined with the lives of others. Unless we have someone who cares for us and for whom we care, it is doubtful that we can or will sustain our lives much longer.

This fact makes questionable the quest for anonymity, that is, the desire to live unknown in our surroundings. We all appreciate privacy, but most of us have too much of it. A careful analysis of the desire for anonymity reveals psychological problems or selfishness. The poet declares that "no man is an island"; and he was right, because the Bible reminds us, "None of us liveth to himself" (Rom. 14:7).

This Thanksgiving season let us thank God for people, for all kinds of people. If there weren't all kinds, then probably no one would love us.

I see intelligent-appearing women with not so intelligent-appearing men, and I ask myself how a woman could love a man like that. And I always answer my questions the same way. I don't know how she can love him, but it's obvious that she does.

I'm sure people wonder why my friends put up with me, but thank God they do! And I'll admit that many of my friends have some peculiar ways, but I like them just the same.

Yes, thank God for people. If we're just trying to get ahead financially instead of making investments in friendship—we're fools! May God help us to realize the real worth of our associations with people. And may we be truly grateful for the tremendous contributions they make to our lives.

II. But if Life Is to Be Meaningful, We Must Feel a Sense of Worth to Ourselves and to Others.

Is someone depending on us? Is what we are spending our time at worth the effort? Thank God for the possibilities

171

of making our lives count. Yes, thank God for freedom—freedom to choose between options. But more than gratitude to our country for our freedoms, let us thank our God for the options. What is freedom if there's nothing to choose? Fortunately God has filled the world with wonderful options—intellectual, environmental, vocational, and spiritual options! We can make our lives what we want them to be. And better yet, we can make them what God planned them to be.

Who on earth has more reason to be grateful than those of us who from childhood have been enlightened by the good news of salvation? Does any material possession compare with the joy of our personal salvation? No, a thousand times, no—nothing compares to the surpassing worth of knowing Christ Jesus as Lord!

So let us, at this Thanksgiving season, be grateful for the things that make a life. And let us not forget that millions are still waiting for that life-giving news about Jesus Christ. Let us commit ourselves to the purpose of giving all men the option of accepting Jesus Christ as Savior and Lord. When we have accomplished that goal, we will have demonstrated our gratitude for the things that make our lives truly whole and satisfying.

Stouthearted Gratitude

SCRIPTURE: John 11:38-44

TEXT: *And Jesus lifted up his eyes, and said, Father, I thank thee that thou hast heard me* (John 11:41*b*).

Is gratitude the compunction of the comfortable? Is it the selfish delight of those who have counted their blessings?

When you have life, health, wealth, friends, and recognition, why not be thankful? But what if the only thing you have is life—and even that is in constant peril? How do you get wound up for Thanksgiving then?

Most of our reasons for gratitude would make little sense to millions of people in this world. It may be easy for people with protruding waistlines to talk about gratitude, but it's tough for people who are starving.

There are millions of people who well might ask, How *in this world* can I be thankful? When we look at the world, the view isn't very encouraging. War and violence devastate the lives of many people. Poverty, starvation, disease, illiteracy, and social evils plague mankind. If you look at the world with this negative view for very long, you will be hard put for gratitude.

So when the going really gets tough, only the life that is established on the biblical concept can face it triumphantly. Others may face it stoically. Many will face it despairingly. But the Christian who has not only believed in Christ but in the biblical explanation of life and destiny can face anything life brings with confidence that victory will ultimately be his. This is not resignation; it is faith.

This kind of faith is the foundation for stouthearted

173

gratitude. It makes it possible for soldiers in combat to find something worthy of gratitude. The impoverished, the ill, and even the outcast can find cause for gratitude. The comfortable man finds the occasion for gratitude not simply in temporal success but in eternal hope.

So as we approach this Thanksgiving Day, let us consider carefully the real causes for gratitude. Let us declare that whatever our lot in life, we have divine reasons for our thankfulness. Let us revel not in the superficialities of life but in the real values of our existence. May our gratitude be stouthearted as we remember the words of Paul. "If God is on our side, who can ever be against us? . . . For I am convinced that nothing can ever separate us from his love. Death can't, and life can't. The angels won't, and all the powers of hell itself cannot keep God's love away. Our fears for today, our worries about tomorrow, or where we are—high above the sky, or in the deepest ocean—nothing will ever be able to separate us from the love of God demonstrated by our Lord Jesus Christ when he died for us" (Rom. 8:31, 38-39, TLB).

Then there are those individuals who are asking how *in their predicament* they can be thankful. They work hard for small wages. One misfortune after another smothers them. Personal and domestic failure hounds them constantly. Disappointment turns into grief and then despair. What a life. Is it worth it? Don't talk to them about gratitude. They'll throw a hunk of reality in the middle of your face!

It's sad to live at the base of a beautiful mountain and not be able to see anything but foothills. But that's the kind of life thousands of people live. All around them is prosperity and pleasure, but all that ever touches them is poverty and sorrow. How *in their predicament* can we expect them to be thankful?

Then there are people like us; healthy, well fed, com-

174

fortable, loved, content. But we have a question about gratitude too. How *in our hearts* can we really be thankful? It's easy to say we are thankful. We can offer all kinds of reasons for being thankful. We can even act thankful. But how can we really feel gratitude in our hearts? How can we possess a deep sense of appreciation and gratefulness for life as we know it? As the poet said,

> He who thanks but with the lips
> Thanks but in part;
> The full, the true Thanksgiving
> Comes from the heart.
>
> (Source unknown)

Is there an answer to the questions confronting us? What about the evil of our world? And what about individual suffering? Can we look these grotesque realities in the face and still feel the balmy breezes of gratitude breathing through our soul? It is possible only if we have a biblical concept of our existence.

I. The First Tenet of a Biblical Concept Is that Life Is a Gift of God.

From the scriptural viewpoint man is not a phenomenon of natural forces. He was made by God and in God's image.

We take life for granted and seldom stop to think what a precious gift it is. When Charles Lindbergh sighted the southern tip of Ireland at the close of his first trans-Atlantic flight, he recorded: "One senses only through change, appreciates only after absence. I haven't been far enough away to know the earth before. For twenty-five years I've lived on it, and yet not seen it till this moment. For nearly two thousand hours, I've flown over it without realizing what wonders lay below. . . . During my entire life I've accepted these gifts of God to man, and not known what

175

was mine until this moment. It's like rain after drought; spring after a northern winter. I've been to eternity and back. I know how the dead would feel to live again."[1]

That's the kind of concept of *life* we need. It makes it much more valuable and precious to us. A concept of life like this will help us be grateful when all we have left is life itself.

II. The Second Tenet of the Biblical Concept of Life Is that Sin Is Responsible for the Suffering and Misery in This World and Our Predicament.

Much of what happens to us is the result of someone's disobedience, selfishness, or immorality. We must understand that suffering is not the venom of fate but the consequence of our own and forbears' actions.

God set this world in motion according to certain physical laws. He doesn't decide each morning whether or not the sun will rise. He established the law regulating the sun when He made the universe. When He created man, God established moral, psychological, and social laws. It is the breaking of these spiritual laws in complex patterns by widely related people that produces the maze of human problems.

III. A Third Tenet of the Biblical Concept of Life Is that "in All Things God Works for the Good of Those Who Love Him" (Rom. 8:28, NIV).

This means that the experiences and circumstances which overwhelm people are not necessarily sent by God. Rather, God is at work on behalf of His people in the midst of their circumstances. Surely He is able to deliver us from every threat of defeat.

---

1. Wallis, *Illus.*, p. 199.

IV. A Fourth Tenet of the Biblical Concept of Life Is that We Have Hope of Everlasting Life.

Someday wrongs will be righted, evil will be condemned. and good will be rewarded. This is no vain rationalization. It is the promise of Jesus Christ.

DALLAS D. MUCCI is the superinten-
dent of the New York District. Prior to
this he was pastor of the South Hills
Church of the Nazarene in Pittsburgh,
Pa., from 1965 to 1980. He is a graduate
of Eastern Nazarene College, 1956, and
Chicago University graduate schools of
History and Pastoral Counseling, 1960
(M.A.). Mr. Mucci pastored Tinley
Park, Ill., Church of the Nazarene be-
fore accepting the Pittsburgh pastor-
ate.

His church offices include a term on
the General Council of the NYPS, and
on the General Board of the Church of
the Nazarene. He is author of *Weekday
Nursery and Kindergarten Schools* and
numerous articles for various Christian
publications.

CHRISTMAS

Dallas D. Mucci

Before "White Christmas" comes the old pop song, "Home for the Holidays"; the mood and atmosphere begin to build. Two weeks before Thanksgiving, Santa Claus drops into the town square or suburban shopping mall—and it is on!

Australians expect to spend Christmas on the beach in the bright, warm glow of summer. North Americans watch the white traces of snow decorate the shriveling goldenrods and hear the cold winds whip the stark naked trees, making the nostalgic "White Christmas" great media stuff every year!

Christmas is a festival of lights, green trees, gift exchanges, special kinds of food by each nationality of our world. Christmas is many sights, sounds, feelings, moods, and even pain for some. It is the season for all from Vladivostok to Bad Axe, Mich.

Yet, Advent has nothing to do with weather, ethnic celebration, food, or area of the world. If Advent has nothing to do with all this memorable and nostalgic living, just what does it have to do with?

For children, it generally means, "Wait!"

"Daddy"—the almost awed look—"Daddy, how many days until Christmas? Is it next Friday?" The agonizing waiting of the children is that admixture of pain and joy, anticipation held in check by a mere calendar.

Older people often experience the opposite, hurried and

sometimes harried days before Christmas. In addition to the shopping pressure is the planned trip or the visit of relatives not seen in many weeks. Then come the Christmas parties, programs, concerts, school activities, church celebrations, and . . .!

These have a bit to do with Advent. However, the waiting and preparation are the twins for a great Advent experience. Why?

I wait again! I prepare again for that great day! I look forward to and want our congregation to look forward to the same 2,000-year-old announcement—Jesus Christ is born in Bethlehem, the city of Judea.

It must always be just like it is happening. The shepherds, the eastern Magi, and angels who are all detailed for us in the Gospels, but are still part of the current Advent. Somehow, we are there or they are here for the Christ who does live in our hearts, who does walk the dusty, joy/grief roads of our lives. So, even at the Advent, our hearts burn within us much as the pair on the Emmaus road!

So, "Joy to the world! the Lord is come" rings out in every heart and church. W. A. Poovey affirmed, "The classic Christmas carol, 'O Little Town of Bethlehem,' says it for us all in the lines, 'The hopes and fears of all the years / Are met in thee tonight.'"

The joy is ours because Christ comes for all seasons and to all people. He comes in redemption and we sing, "O come, O come, Emmanuel, / And ransom captive Israel."

Now, as we prepare and wait, our knowledge of the First Advent kindles our hope for His second coming. The astounding truth of the First Advent promises the Second Advent! "You ought to live holy and godly lives as you look forward to the day of God and speed its coming" (2 Pet. 3: 11b-12a, NIV).

So in the midst of the human celebration, waiting and hectic, blessed and wearing, the pattern of Advent should be the preparation of hearts to Christ! That is the only preparation that the church should make!

The Advent is Christmas! Christmas Eve should be celebration rather than material exchange. The light that has shone out of darkness should dominate the celebration.

For Christians, the New Year doesn't really begin on January 1; instead, it begins four Sundays before. Advent is the beginning of the Christian year. It is the beginning because the celebration causes every Christian to remember again that God in Christ reached out to all men. There is no other way for a Christian to start a new year. Or is there?

The Bible does not mention Advent, Lent, or set certain days on the church calendar. However, the proclamation of the gospel came through a church which was scattered but still lived in spite of persecution.

In their living the good news, it was not a religious or philosophical idea! It was not a debate about moral concepts, but they were living out the saving deeds of Jesus Christ. It is little wonder that the Early Church began to set aside days to celebrate. Every reminder was a blessing!

Advent is a glorious celebration when it is in Christ!

Matthew's Christmas Message

SCRIPTURE: Matthew, chapters 1 and 2

Matthew's Christmas message has a gap between chapters 1 and 2, like the silent night. His message is more events than word concepts like John. Included in his chapters 1 and 2, there are the genealogies, story of the Magi, and then the terrible slaughter and suffering and the flight of Jesus and His parents.

Matthew's shrill discords over against Luke's sweet harmonies force us into looking differently at the birth of Christ. Jesus didn't come into a hospitable world! Did Jesus come to bring peace or a sword, or both? Matthew's emphasis on the Virgin Birth has caused moderns to speculate, "Just maybe this whole thing is a myth."

Others complain! It doesn't really fit—all the angels, dreams, and miracles. With all the great fascination these really aren't quite true, are they? Their hearts hear the gospel, but their minds are still excluded!

God's power stands at the threshold of this narrative, sifting the readers—who believe they are sifting the text!

Matthew gives the entrance of the Christ child and at the same time the admission or rejection of those attracted by Christ. Luke records the power of the Child with his record of the adoration of the shepherds and of Simeon and Anna.

Matthew shows us the people who are being sifted.

I. We Watch the Magi.

Matthew gives this single instance of the Magi. We watch them as they ride into Jerusalem, the three "heathen" men of Persia, the star watchers. These men were admitted to God's revelation. But first they had to meet another "King of the Jews," Herod. At that meeting Herod shows us the contrast. The Magi would follow the light that had shined out of darkness, but Herod will try to use the light for personal political gain.

The Magi, "when they saw the star, they were overjoyed" (Matt. 2:10, NIV). It led them to the house in Bethlehem where Mary and Jesus were living. They were so overjoyed that they bowed down and worshiped. Expression of their joy was full when they gave the symbolic gifts of gold, incense, and myrrh.

182

Again, we see that God speaks to men who will listen. The Magi are warned of Herod's designs in a dream and slip away by another route. Herod waits but gets no message from them.

II. We Watch Herod.

Herod not only represents the irritability and selfishness of all human tyrants; he also illustrates the background of Jesus' life; namely, the cruelty and pettiness of Herod's rule under Rome. Israel was torn from within and no spiritual direction could be found. Herod's slaughter in Bethlehem is a horrible illustration of the terror that also reigned!

King Herod pretended to share the common hope for peace, but as soon as the light of Christ appeared, he felt compelled to destroy Him. This is always true. Matthew is helping us to understand the entrance of light into darkness. God is sifting with His offer of grace.

The terrible rage of Herod shows his helplessness. He kills thousands of innocent people to keep his power. It is always this way in the darkness of Satan. People are expendable for power or material wealth.

In the end, the light could not be destroyed. God may withdraw. But Jesus' flight to Egypt was only a temporary one.

Soon Herod was dead!

III. We Watch the People.

The screen of history flickers to silence on the Magi and Herod, and we have seen the drama of the birth of Christ via Matthew's report.

The light of Christ has come to all men at Bethlehem and calls to us, Come from darkness to light.

Some will respond, How can I love in a cruel world? Step aside so that I may carve out my place. Don't you know that if you don't carve it out, you'll be done in? How helpless!

Others will bow down and worship! Out of their treasure will be offered the gold and incense of a life to be molded in loving, holy service. In their weakness is the strength of Christ.

Where are you this first Sunday of Advent? In the darkness of power or the light of God's love?

Joseph and Us

SCRIPTURE: Matt. 1:20-21, NIV: *She will give birth to a son, and you are to give him the name Jesus, because he will save his people from their sins.*

In 1976 a movie was almost filmed in England that would have made Christ a lurid, rather pathetic figure. The next year a pseudohistorical book was published at Eastertide called *The Passover Plot.* All pointed to unbelief concerning the divinity of Christ. This is nothing new!

In Matthew's Gospel Joseph was confronted with the same dilemma: Jesus, Son of God and son of David!

One day Joseph, engaged to be married, discovered that Mary, his bride-to-be, was expecting a child. In their culture an engagement was binding. But more astounding was Mary's story of the visit of an angel. Could he believe what this angel told Mary? A child both God and man! How?

He did have alternatives. He could have a public trial to exonerate himself, but it would disgrace Mary. So, he must have thought of a private trial with two witnesses, and quietly moving her to live with a relative.

Suddenly, we see in Joseph the issue before the whole world. Who is Jesus? The son of David or the Son of God? Would you believe—both!

Joseph, called a righteous man in Matt. 1:19, had to be concerned about the birth of a child. He was torn in a great struggle with the forces of his own nature; hurt pride fighting against his love for Mary, and anger struggling with self-control.

It was resolved (Matt. 1:19, NIV): Joseph would divorce Mary quietly. Before he could act, an angel of the Lord appeared to him in a dream and gave Joseph the same message that Mary had been told.

Joseph is told that Mary's future motherhood is the will and work of God. God is, through this simple, righteous, harried carpenter and his young bride-to-be, saying, I want you to be an instrument for the eternal goal of creation: *salvation of man.*

Now Joseph knows. He arises from his sleep a new man. Maturity has brought determination and understanding until he accepts his role.

For us this is Joseph's lesson: Understanding that we are in Joseph's position, facing the stumbling block—Is Jesus the son of David and the Son of God?

Whenever a person is born again, it is by faith. Not that faith saves. But unless faith breaks through the walls of pride, seen in scientific and material achievement, seen in our own sensible righteousness, seen in our own knowledge of life, in a painful crisis, there will be no new life!

Always the Joseph question: "Who is Christ?" The question restated by Christ to His disciples: "Whom do men say that I am?" (Matt. 16:13).

When we know, in faith, there is no apology; Christ, supernatural, was conceived by the Holy Spirit!

With Dag Hammarskjöld, "God does not die on the day when we cease to believe in a personal God, but we die on the day our lives cease to be illuminated by the steady radiance."

Then let's go as Joseph to:

1. Accept our role as witnesses.
2. Live in a supernatural faith.
3. Expect the surprises of God.

Zechariah and His Vision

SCRIPTURE: Luke 1:5-20

Waiting is an Old Testament emphasis and something we moderns detest. Perhaps our prayer lives are almost "fast-hit" monologues because we hate to wait! But Advent was the culmination of waiting.

The waiting of Zechariah, father of John the Baptist, is a good Christmas model.

I. It Is a Picture of the Soul Waiting for God.

The emphasis of the old priest was "My soul waiteth for the Lord more than they that watch for the morning" (Ps. 130:6). It is good that a man should both quietly wait and hope for the salvation of the Lord! Zechariah and Elizabeth waited for a son. In their hardpressed waiting, one thing was bright and real—their faith in a living God! It is easy to consent to God's will when the command is to act. But faith is tested when we are told to wait, to pray, and to look up. In the words of the Psalmist, "Be still, and know that I am God" (Ps. 46:10).

II. The Passage Before Us Reveals the Hearer of Prayer.

In verse 13, "Your prayer has been heard" (NIV). Was this the prayer for the son? Or was it the priestly prayer offered at the altar for the hope and salvation of Israel? Both may be included. For in the two scriptural instances the yearning for a son, the blessing for the individual, is associated with the blessing to the whole Church of God. The prayer of faith has interconnections with the purposes of God far beyond our power to estimate. Matthew Henry quaintly writes, "Prayers are filed in heaven, and are not forgotten though things prayed for in the present are not given to us. The time as well as the 'thing' is the answer; and God's gift always transcends the measure of promise."

III. Let's See the Reality of the Spiritual World.

If we aren't careful, we make our world so different. The natural world is the natural world and God must stay out. The spiritual world is the spiritual and God is in there!

Our world must be really different with the natural and spiritual pressed and interwoven together.

Why should it seem unbelievable that Gabriels and Michaels should at God's bidding deliver messages or provide help?

It isn't if God is truly involved in the whole of our world! Scripture tells us that the very hairs of our head are numbered; that's how much God cares.

Then one could say, where there is a praying heart there is the angel "at the right side of the altar of incense" (Luke 1:11, NIV).

IV. Belief Always Necessary.

Punishment is one of many warnings in Scripture against unbelief. Unbelief is the only limiting of the Holy One of Israel. The same questions from Zechariah are such as come from many: "How can I be sure of this? I am an old man and my wife is well along in years" (v. 18, NIV). "How shall I know when?" is the type of question that arises in our hearts. The good priest had waited long, but his moment of unbelief cost him.

He had been told to wait a bit longer, and his punishment of silence made all the more painful the waiting.

But God is never thwarted in His reaching out to His lost sheep. Let's be part of those who pray, wait, see, and are part of the salvation of the Lord as we celebrate the Advent, Christmas.

Christmas: Gifts or Gift?

(Possible Christmas Eve message)

SCRIPTURE: Luke 1:46-55

Our life has a grimness to it. Amidst plenty, I hear the voices of uncertainty, boredom, and a sense of almost defeat. Crises of energy, morals, and fear of the future punctuate most thinking, until our world tremblingly fumbles along in at least semidarkness. Conflict and clash are the answers, rather than conciliation and compassion in this atmosphere.

Talented, able, and still rich, but one of history's most violent peoples are we Americans. Often the whole thing erupts into one of those little brushfire wars with a lone, tormented soldier of fortune striking out at a loved one—brother, wife, or even parent. Or another soldier strikes out at the society.

Herod's legacy of the days before Christ mirrors the serious crisis of our lives. Our technocrats call out to God with our instructions for Him. In fact, God's instruction of moral virtue and humility are relegated to outmoded, dead concepts.

Our society has replaced virtue, if we ever had much, with the acquisition of things. Somehow, the crisis is lost on many of us in the consuming desire to possess goods in abundance. The visions in our children's heads during this Christmas is a long list of things.

This very vision is a major reason for the violence in our society. When spiritual values are still loudly proclaimed, but relegated actually to holiday speeches and sermons, violence is one result. When consumption and abundance of things is a key virtue, violence is the only way to achieve it for many. This is true of nations as well as individual persons.

But this night of miracles—Christmas night! We are jerked from our failing world to an exciting life that calls for compassion, humility, and a willingness to renounce all the trinkets that brings the violence.

In Luke's record of Mary's joy, the Magnificat, we understand that the source of living is God.

I. Mary Recognized in Her Selection the Condescending Love of God.

She sees herself not a person to be exalted. Her adoration is unbounded: "My soul praises the Lord and my spirit rejoices in God my Savior" (Luke 1:46-47, NIV). In her whole song she sees the living God stooping to man in his need. Man does not have to live in fear, but is called to know the joy of God's involvement in the world.

II. Spiritual Life Is Just That!

The everlasting joy is the incarnate God with us—God who will meet man at the point of need and then transform the man. God's answer to violence is not a treatise, but a loving gift and the transforming power of the Holy Spirit.

Saul left Jerusalem breathing out threats and slaughters against that religious sect, and then he met Jesus. Later he wrote, "Let nothing be done through strife or vainglory; but in lowliness of mind let each esteem other better than themselves" (Phil. 2:3).

Augustine was satiated on the decadent sex madness of Rome, heard the incarnate Christ, then moved from lust and violence to compassion and concern.

Malcolm Muggeridge, the great English satirist, poked fun and wrought some mayhem in most circles. Suddenly his book *Jesus Rediscovered* appeared, recounting his encounter with Christ. Now Muggeridge speaks of hope in a world that for him had been hopeless.

All these understand Mary's song.

Christmas is the Good News—it is the enlightening hope of Christ, alive in us in our world.

In Martin Luther's *Meditation on the Gospels*, he tells the episode at the Council of Constance.

> A cardinal went for a ride in the field and saw there a peasant weeping. The cardinal, being a kind man, did not wish to ride by, and so stopped to comfort the man. The peasant wept for a long time and would say nothing, so that the cardinal worried about him. Then the peasant pointed to a toad and said, "I am weeping because God made me such a fine creature and not ugly like the toad, and yet I have never acknowledged His gifts with thanks and praise."

Then the cardinal was so smitten that he fell from his horse and had to be carried to a house. When he regained his senses, he said, "O Augustine, how well have you said, 'The unlettered rise up and take heaven before us, and we with all our skills wallow in flesh and blood.'"

O my heart doth magnify the Lord!

HAROLD BONNER is pastor of the First Church of the Nazarene, Auburn, Calif., where he has served since 1973. A graduate of Pasadena College and of Nazarene Theological Seminary, his previous pastoral career has been in California with congregations in Oakland, San Anselmo, Los Angeles Highland Park, and Alhambra. In addition to his pastoral duties he has served as District Church Schools chairman, District Advisory Board member, lecturer in philosophy and religion at Pasadena College, and is currently serving as district secretary. He has compiled two volumes published by Nazarene Publishing House, *Proclaiming the Spirit* and *Proclaiming the Savior*.

FUNERALS

Harold Bonner

The declaring of the good news of the gospel in the setting of the funeral is a ministry that is challenging, demanding, and rewarding. It is not easy to "mourn with those who mourn" (Rom. 12:15, NIV); it never was meant to be. But how fulfilling it is to be used of the Holy Spirit to bring the sense of the eternal God into the dark hours of human loss—to affirm that in Jesus Christ there is life that death can never, never destroy.

Each pastor is unique and will mature into his own ministerial expression. For myself, there have been three major lessons that have shaped my understanding of preaching in the funeral setting. The first and most important is that of *responsibility*. When I faced conducting my first funeral during my last year of seminary, a classmate wisely shared with me: "The one thing to remember about conducting the funeral service is, *you are it.*" How true. As is true of no other public service, in the funeral the pastor is the service. He carries that responsibility and cannot be excused from it. What he is, the service becomes—his dignity, his faith, his love, his concern, his walk with God. That is why the funeral service takes so much out of the minister. In that hour of death, he has entered into that experience of loss and stood strong and tall to point lives to Him who is the Way, the Truth, and the Life.

The second lesson has been that of *appropriateness*. Every death is a loss in the human family. And every funeral

193

service is a time for seriousness and dignity. But every funeral must have its own proper focus if the ministry is to be effective. The grief focus will be more dominant in a funeral for the victim of a tragic accident than it will be in the death of an older person after a long illness. The atmosphere of triumphant victory will befit the home going of the saint of God, but hardly is it appropriate for the wasted life of an unbeliever. How important it is to fine-tune one's funeral ministry to the occasion.

The third lesson has to do with *personalness.* By that I do not mean a chattiness that would rob the funeral service of that quiet dignity that enables the Holy Spirit to do His work in the guarded privacy of each heart. I rather mean a warm awareness of the bereaved family that at some point in the service ministers just to them. Some years ago tragedy struck the family of a close friend. Rev. George Taylorson, then pastor of the Bresee Church of the Nazarene in Pasadena, Calif., conducted the memorial service which was attended by several hundred people. At the conclusion of his message he turned to the family, seated together, and said something like this:

"And to the members of the family, may I commend the memories that are yours alone—memories of love and family, and life that was shared so meaningfully. May these memories be sanctified for your blessing in the days ahead.

"And, secondly, may I commend to you the presence of this company of people who have gathered with you today and who say by their coming that they care, that they love you, and that their lives are touched by your loss.

"And, lastly, may I commend to you the grace of our Lord Jesus Christ, and the love of God our Father, and the present ministry of the Holy Spirit, who is here today to walk with you with strength and comfort into your unknown tomorrows." Those words ministered to me that day, and ever since then I have closed each funeral message with some adaptation of them.

For most funeral occasions I have found the following sequence appropriate: Scripture readings; invocation; eulogy; hymn (either sung or played); message; benediction. While the funeral message is not lengthy, it is still the major segment of the memorial service. It is a time for the positive statement of the great truth of our Christian faith. What follows are four such messages that have seemed to me to be fitting and effective in the memorial service setting.

The God Who Says, "Come"

TEXT: *Come unto me, all ye that labour and are heavy laden, and I will give you rest. Take my yoke upon you, and learn of me; for I am meek and lowly in heart: and ye shall find rest unto your souls. For my yoke is easy, and my burden is light* (Matt. 11:28-30).

In the losses and hurts of our human journey, it is the Word of the eternal God that speaks to us with authority and with power. These words from Jesus Christ have been across the centuries a never failing well of strength and renewal. Let us listen to them again in this memorial hour, and let us lay hold on the truth they affirm, the grace they offer.

I. God's Word Is "Come."

This verse reminds us of that. God's word is "Come." Indeed, it is His favorite word. It is the word that keeps repeating through the Scripture, and it is the last word of the last book of His written Word to us, the Bible: "And the Spirit and the bride say, Come. And let him that heareth say, Come. And let him that is athirst come. And whosoever will, let him take the water of life freely" (Rev. 22:17).

It is God's great word to all mankind in general and each person individually. "*Come* unto me, all ye that labour and are heavy laden."

It is God's great word because mankind in general and each man specifically fumbles and stumbles through life, searching proudly for life in ways that never lead to life. It was the prophet Isaiah who rightly described our plight: "Wherefore do ye spend money for that which is not bread? and your labour for that which satisfieth not? . . . Ho, every one that thirsteth, come ye to the waters" (55:2, 1).

"Come" is God's great word because of His great love for all of us. It was the observation of the sainted Augustine who said, "Thou hast made us for thyself, O God, and our souls are restless until they find their rest in Thee." And so He works, and so He speaks to draw us to himself—seeking us, pursuing us, whispering in the quiet hours, "Come." It is our hope.

II. God's Way Is Jesus.

The God who says, "Come," has told us the way by which we do come to Him. It is Jesus Christ, the Son of God become the Son of Man that sons of men might become sons of God. It is He who speaks for God, "Come." It is He who points the way, "Come unto me." The eternal God is not difficult. He has come to us on our territory, within our limitations. He gave His Son in order that we might become His children. He said of Jesus that He was all we needed to find Him, and in Him, find ourselves. For Jesus is the Way, the Truth, the Life (John 14:6). He is, indeed, the way to the Father.

196

The testimony of those who come to God through Jesus Christ is that they find Him. In Him they find life's great hunger satisfied and life's great rest tasted—delivering their feet from falling, their eyes from tears, their souls from death (see Ps. 116:8). And their affirmation calls us to follow faithfully that way of God, even Jesus.

III. God's Time Is Now.

The word is present tense. "Come"—come, now. God's come is always present tense. Today, in this hour of loss; now, with this aching burden, "Come." He does not say, "Come," in the past tense, for none of us can go back and undo or change. He does not say, "Come," in some future situation. We do not live there.

How kind is our Heavenly Father. He comes to us— wherever we are, and whoever we are—and says, "Come," and do it right now, just as you are—and find all that you need in Me. And that we can do, even here, in these moments and in this place.

IV. God's Gift Is Himself.

"Come unto me . . . and I will give you rest." Not just a momentary breath of relief, but a whole new life through Jesus Christ, and in Him, a life that even death can never, never destroy. Because God's gift is himself—His life—because of that great truth He gives a peace that burdens cannot crush and a fellowship with Him that cannot be broken. For this He made us; for this we hunger; and all of this we find, as we come to Him through Jesus Christ—and do it just now. Said some unknown poet:

> My goal is God himself—not joy, nor peace,
> Nor even blessing, but himself, my Lord.
> 'Tis His to lead me there, not mine, but His,
> At any cost, dear Lord, by any road.

197

So faith bounds forward to its goal in God,
  And love can trust her Lord to lead her there.
Upheld by Him, my soul is following hard
  Till God hath fulfilled my deepest prayer.

No matter if the way be sometimes dark;
  No matter though the cost be ofttimes great;
He knoweth best how I can reach the mark:
  The path that leads to Him must needs be straight.

One thing I know, I cannot say Him nay.
  One thing I do, I press towards my Lord;
My God, my glory here, from day to day,
  And in the glory there, my great Reward.

The God Who Waits to Be Known

TEXT: *Behold, I stand at the door, and knock: if any man hear my voice, and open the door, I will come in to him, and will sup with him, and he with me* (Rev. 3:20).

We would be less than human today if there were no sharp pain of sorrow because one we have loved deeply is now suddenly gone from us. But we would be less than Christian if in the midst of this memorial hour there were not also the strong notes of triumphant faith in God through Jesus Christ. The Scripture says, "Precious in the sight of the Lord is the death of his saints" (Ps. 116:15). Life's highest achievement is not gold which perishes, nor fame which fades so quickly. Life's highest achievement is to know Him, from whom not even death can separate us. That is the victory of faith; it is the victory that belonged to him whose passing brings us together today.

Out of the treasured passage of Rev. 3:20 let me share

with you three possible relationships with God through Christ Jesus our Lord.

I. The First Possible Relationship Is Christ the Stranger to Our Lives.

The concept of a stranger is the opening phrase of this verse—"Behold, I stand at the door." This is where the script of every man's life begins, with Christ outside the door of his soul. This is what the Bible means by the fall of man. This is the picture of sin—God on the outside of our lives rather than at home in our hearts. This is the root of man's anxiety, why he is "lonely and afraid in a world he never made." The God who made man for himself is on the outside, a stranger to him.

A. But the Stranger knocks. That is the hope of man. Not everyone opens the door of his life to His transforming fellowship. Some are annoyed by the Stranger's call. They drown out His rapping by the louder sounds of ambition and pleasure. Some never seem to understand that He is really there, at the door of their life, offering himself and all that comes with Him—life eternal and life abundant. Some peak through the tiny window in the door of the human spirit and, seeing that it is the Lord who is calling, withdraw from Him in guilt and fear. They do not invite Him in, as Francis Thompson put it, "lest having Him, they have nothing else besides."

B. When Holman Hunt painted his famous picture of *Christ at the Door*, he captured the truth so well. The door of the human heart has no outside knob. It only opens from within. No one, not even the Son of God, can force His way in. And so long as He is on the outside, He is a stranger to us, and we are strangers to His transforming love and fellowship. Said the hymn writer, J. B. Atchison, so perceptively:

There's a Stranger at the door,
 Let Him in:
He has been there oft before,
 Let Him in.
Let Him in, ere He is gone,
Let Him in, the Holy One,
Jesus Christ, the Father's Son,
 Let Him in.

II. The Second Possible Relationship Is Christ the Guest of Our Lives.

Notice how the verse develops: "Behold, I stand at the door, and knock; if any man hear my voice, and open the door, I will come in to him, and will sup with him."

Blessed are they that let that Stranger in, and come to know Him, Jesus Christ, the blessed Savior. When He enters the life, what a difference He makes! He brings a peace with God and a peace with ourselves. He brings a confidence in the eternal here in the conflicts of time. Well does the Scripture say, "Christ in you, the hope of glory" (Col. 1:27).

This is the beginning of that for which we are made. And every person I have known who has invited Him into his life has said, "This is the best thing I have ever done."

But notice that when we invite the eternal God in Christ Jesus into our lives, He comes as our Guest. He sits at our table. We are the ones making the plans. We are the ones in charge. When we are at our best, we seek to make our Heavenly Guest happy. But when we are pressured or weary, then the presence of a guest, even the Heavenly Guest, can become a kind of burden till we act as if we wish He were not there.

That is why the Bible never presents the idea of Jesus as the Guest of our lives as the goal of our relationship with God.

III. The Third Possible Relationship Is Christ the Master of Our Lives.

The full passage reads: "Behold, I stand at the door, and knock: if any man hear my voice, and open the door, I will come in to him, and will sup with him, and he with me." The phrasing is not accidental; it is intentional. For if we permit Him to work out His plan in us, it will always be that the One we have welcomed as Guest will proceed to be crowned as Master—a full confidence in His authority and a full commitment to His will.

At the marriage of Cana in Galilee, Jesus was only a guest (John 2:1-11). But then the banquet was threatened. And Jesus the Guest became Jesus the Host, with power to transform. What a difference He then made.

On the evening of the Resurrection, two discouraged Christians walked the lonely road to Emmaus (Luke 24: 13-35). A stranger walked with them, explained the Cross to them, and was invited into their home by them. But at that table the Guest became the Host; He broke bread to them, and then it was they knew Him. Then it was that the risen Lord made the difference.

What is the high goal of life? It is to know Him—surely not as Stranger, and not even as Guest. The goal of life is to know Him, Jesus Christ our Lord, as the saving Master and living Lord of our lives.

Here, in the midst of these memorial moments, He waits for us to open to Him.

The Call of Jesus

TEXT: *Let not your heart be troubled: ye believe in God, believe also in me. In my Father's house are many mansions: if it were not so, I would have told you. I go to prepare a place for you. And if I go and prepare a place for you, I will come again, and receive you unto myself; that where I am, there ye may be also* (John 14:1-3).

In this hour of death when once more we are keenly aware of the limitations of our human wisdom and strength, we turn to our Lord for that understanding that is so much greater than our own. We have not gathered today to hear the words of man; that helps us but little. We have gathered to sense again the Voice of the Eternal, declaring again with power, "The world passeth away . . . but he that doeth the will of God abideth for ever" (1 John 2:17).

That message from God we discover in the treasured words of our Lord Jesus in John 14. Think on them with me today. They tell us of the call of Jesus.

I. The Word of Jesus Is a Call to Believe.

Jesus said, "Believe on me" (v. 1). It is both strong command and tender invitation. What nobility of life there is in earnest believing on the Savior—strong and sure. The best things in life, both *here* and *hereafter*, come out of the decision to believe on Jesus and crown Him as the living Lord of Life.

William Barclay has observed that there are really only two moments in a person's life that matter ultimately. The first is the moment when he is born; the second is the moment when he discovers *why* he was born. The first is the

moment of the flesh; the second is a moment of the spirit—
an awakening that comes as we commit ourselves to Him, a
new birth of the spirit that charges life with meaning and
opens up the gates of life eternal.

We are deeply taught by our gathering today that our
hold on life is fragile—possessions may be lost; relationships
may be broken; this life itself snatched from us as by a thief
in the night.

But the child of God is taught by the Word of God that
his one secure possession is God in Jesus Christ the Lord.
Not even death can separate us from Him (Rom. 8:38-39).
And He becomes ours by the simple yet life-changing act of
believing on Him.

"Believe in me," Jesus directed—not as a last resort, but
as life's one sure hope. As George Matheson wrote, so let
us do and affirm:

> O Love that wilt not let me go,
> I rest my weary soul in Thee.
> I give Thee back the life I owe,
> That in Thine ocean depths its flow
>   May richer, fuller be.

II. The Word of Jesus Is a Call to Purpose.

Jesus said, "I go to prepare a place for you" (v. 2)—for
you who believe in Me. What meaning *that life* adds to
this life.

There are so many things that we do not understand.
We can do no other than ask, "Why?"—"Why can tragedy
so suddenly cast the gloom of darkness on a Thursday afternoon?" The answers to our "whys" do not come quickly.

But in this hour let us be strengthened by the confidence that our Lord never loses sight of us. These years here,
be they few or many, in His good plan are only prelude.
Jesus said He was preparing a place for those that love Him.

And in the meantime He is preparing those that love Him for that place.

The power to live nobly in a hard and often disappointing world is found in the knowledge that faith and obedience and integrity bear an eternal reward. When a person knows of an inheritance on the other side, he can endure untold hardships on this side.

Jesus said, "I go to prepare a place for *you*." By faith in Him, place your name in that company.

III. The Word of Jesus Is a Call to Continued Fellowship.

Notice how this passage concludes: "And if I go and prepare a place for you, I will come again, and receive you unto myself; that where I am, there ye may be also" (v. 3).

It is a profound thing that we may discover our strongest affirmations of life in the solemn hours of death, when we reach out to find a foundation more solid than the ones that are crumbling around us. That foundation is Jesus Christ our Lord, and in Him, a life that death cannot destroy—a fellowship that endures the brighter in God's eternal heaven. Continued fellowship, that is His call; that is His promise. Will you take hold of it today? Here in this hour that speaks so much of yesterday, will you lay hold of God's great tomorrow?

Fanny Crosby has put this confidence into words:

> *Someday the silver cord will break,*
> *And I no more as now shall sing.*
> *But, oh, the joy when I shall wake*
> *Within the palace of the King!*
>
> *Someday my earthly house will fall;*
> *I cannot tell how soon 'twill be.*
> *But this I know—my All in All*
> *Has now a place in heav'n for me.*

The Crown of Righteousness

TEXT: *I have fought a good fight, I have finished my course, I have kept the faith: henceforth there is laid up for me a crown of righteousness, which the Lord, the righteous judge, shall give me at that day: and not to me only, but unto all them also that love his appearing* (2 Tim. 4:7-8).

None of us dreamed last week we would be here in this memorial chapel today. But for this hour our fellow Christian made ready long ago and settled her account with God. Across the years Jesus has been both personal Savior and Friend. In recent weeks as physical decline was upon her, she spoke frequently of wanting the Lord to take her home. Some of her last words to me concerned this time and this gathering. Death did not take her unprepared. She was ready.

The words of the apostle Paul seem so appropriate to her life and this occasion, for she too could affirm, "I have fought a good fight, I have finished my course, I have kept the faith." Think with me around those words.

I. Everyone Must Say, "I Have Finished My Course."

We are reminded by our gathering here that the days of our lives are limited. They may be many, or they may be few, but swiftly the course of time runs out. We may extend them a little by our carefulness or shorten them greatly by our foolishness. But nothing we can do can change the fact that the earthly life of each one of us is moving toward the moment when each of us must say—in fact, if not in word, "It is done."

It is the universal human tendency to think that sudden

205

misfortune happens only to the other fellow; and to think of ourselves that we have plenty of time. We may; we may not. The writer of Proverbs was so wise when he wrote: "Boast not thyself of to morrow; for thou knowest not what a day may bring forth" (27:1). Tomorrows are never guaranteed. Wise is the man who keeps his relationships both with God and man up to date. For somewhere, someplace, sometime, the sands of time run out.

II. Many May Say, "I Have Fought a Good Fight."

The glory of human life is found in the freedom and ability to choose the high road rather than the low road. And there are many, who, knowing life's days are numbered, determine to make them worthwhile and noble. They seek earnestly to leave footprints that cause no man to stumble, and that are instead markers for a better way.

All of us are debtors to this company. We have benefited from their wisdom and have been lifted by their touch upon this world for good. How brutish life would be without them.

III. But It Is the Redeemed of the Lord Who Alone Can Say, "I Have Kept the Faith."

Faithful Christians can say they have kept the faith, and their lives testify to it with a life-changing glory and witness. And this is the highest achievement of all. This is the one that God has declared swings open wide the gates of life eternal. And this is the testimony of our fellow Christian: "I have kept the faith; I have made my life His life, and His mine. Death may change my place of *residence*, but it cannot and will not change my *ownership*. I am my Lord's and He is mine."

The child of God knows that he has here no continuing city. But he also knows that he has a sure hope and a certain goal. He has set his eyes and heart on Jesus, and from Him he will not turn back. He is sure that no matter what the cost of following Jesus here may be, He is worth it all. For in Jesus, the best is yet to be. Like the apostle Paul, he has fixed his claim, through grace, on the crown of righteousness bestowed by the hand of God, the righteous Judge.

This is the Christian confidence that undergirds this act of memorial today. One we have loved, and now lost for a while, has been received by her Lord into His eternal city of heaven. We are impoverished by her absence. But we have been touched by her life for God and good. We lift our praise. She has fought a good fight; she has finished her course; she has kept the faith; she has received the crown of life. With Charles Wesley we say:

> *Servant of God, well done.*
> *Thy glorious warfare's past.*
> *The battle's fought, the race is run;*
> *And thou art crowned at last.*

Index of Texts